I0436787

Ethnic Emails

The Jewish Connection

Collected by Dr. Alan G. Greene & Arnold A. Kramer

authorHOUSE®

AuthorHouse™
1663 Liberty Drive, Suite 200
Bloomington, IN 47403
www.authorhouse.com
Phone: 1-800-839-8640

© 2008 Collected by Dr. Alan G. Greene & Arnold A. Kramer. All rights reserved.

No part of this book may be reproduced, stored in a retrieval system, or transmitted by any means without the written permission of the author.

First published by AuthorHouse 6/25/2008

ISBN: 978-1-4343-6626-9 (sc)

Printed in the United States of America
Bloomington, Indiana

This book is printed on acid-free paper.

Dedicated to our wives and children and with a nod to those old-time tummelers in the Catskills

Other Collections by Dr. Alan Greene

Through the Years...: A Collection of E-mail Jokes, Random Thoughts and Other Funny Stuff

Acknowledgments

There are many people who have contributed to the stories and pictures that follow. It is not possible to be sure of the origins of the following tales and pictures, but the group that we can most readily identify are: Jules Schwartz, Richard Ellis, Jane and Mitch Weingrad, Warren Mitofsky, Dan Gould, David Berger, Bernie Shuster, Al Simon, David Talman and Manny Rotenberg.

To all these and to any others who had a hand in passing these tales and pictures along we want to express our ever grateful thanks

Foreword

Ethnic jokes are fairly universal, and often interchangeable. One has only to insert a group name (Poles, Mexicans, Texas Aggies, blondes) in the punch line to make a joke refer to a specific group. In Brazil, for example, they would tell the same stories, frequently called "Polish jokes" or "Texas Aggie jokes", and substitute European Portuguese in the punch line.

Some jokes are group specific i.e.:

> Q.-What is black and blue and floats face down in the Monongahela River?

> A.-Someone who tells Polish jokes in Pittsburgh.

And then there are stories that either focus on or exaggerate ethnic traits.

Hope you enjoy the following and don't get upset.

If at any time you want to use a Middle European Yiddish accent, feel free.

Some of the stories you may have heard, but we are sure that many of the stories you haven't.

A very orthodox, heavily bearded, Hasidic man arranges for a hooker to come to his room for the evening. Once in the room, they undress, climb into bed, and go at it.

When finished, the Hasid jumps up, runs over to a window takes a deep breath, runs through a door, comes back, jumps back into bed with the hooker and repeats the performance.

The hooker is impressed with the gusto of the second encounter. When finished, the Hasid jumps up, runs over to the window, takes a deep breath, runs through a door, comes back, jumps back into bed with the hooker and starts again.

The hooker is amazed as this sequence is repeated four times.

During the fifth encore, she decides to try it herself. So, when they are done, she jumps up, goes to the window, takes a deep breath, runs through the door, and finds…

The other nine members of the minyan.

*   *   *   *   *

Yiddish is a combination of German and Phlegm.

*   *   *   *   *

Then there was the dyslexic Rabbi that went around saying, "Yo."

New Jewish Words

1. JEWBILATION n. Pride in finding out that one's favorite celebrity is Jewish.

2. TORAHFIED n. Inability to remember one's lines when called to read from the Torah at one's Bar or Bat mitzvah.

3. SANTA-SHMANTA n. The explanation Jewish children get for why they celebrate Hanukah while the rest of the neighbors celebrate Christmas.

4. MATZILATION v. Smashing a piece of matzo to bits while trying to butter it.

5. BUBBEGUM n. Candy one's mother gives to her grandchildren that she never gave to her own children.

6. CHUTZPAPA n. A father who wakes his wife at 4:00 a.m. so she can change the baby's diaper.

7. DEJA NU n. Having the feeling you've seen the same exasperated look on your mother's face but not knowing exactly when.

8. DISORIYENTA n. When Aunt Sadie gets lost in a department store and strikes up a conversation with everyone she passes.

9. GOYFER n. A Gentile messenger.

10. HEBORT vb. To forget all the Hebrew one ever learned immediately after one's Bar Mitzvah.

11. JEWDO n. A traditional form of self defense based on talking one's way out of a tight spot.

12. MAMATZAH BALLS n. Matzo balls that are as good as mother used to make.

13. MEINSTEIN – slang. "My son, the genius."

14. MISHPOCHADOTS n. The assorted lipstick and make-up stains found on one's face and collar after kissing all one's aunts and cousins at a reception.

15. RE-SHTETLEMENT n. Moving from Brooklyn to Miami and finding all your old neighbors live in the same condo building as you.

16. ROSH HASHANA-NA-NA n. A rock 'n roll band from Brooklyn.

17. YIDENTIFY v. To be able to determine ethnic origins of celebrities even though their names might be St. John, Davis, or Taylor.

18. MINYASTICS n. Going to incredible lengths and troubles to find a tenth person to complete a minyan.

19. FEELAWFUL n. Indigestion from eating Israeli street food.

20. DIS-KVELLIFIED vb. To drop out of law school, med. school or business school as seen through the eyes of parents, grandparents, and Uncle Sid. In extreme cases, simply choosing to major in art history when Irv's son, David, is majoring in biology, is sufficient grounds for diskvellification.

21. IMPASTA n. A Jew who starts eating leavened foods before the end of Passover.

22. KINDERS SHLEP v. To transport other kids in your car besides yours.

23. SCHMUCKLUCK n. Finding out one's wife became pregnant after one's vasectomy.

24. SHOFARSOGUT n. The relief you feel when after many attempts the shofar is finally blown at the end of Yom Kippur.

25. TRAYFFIC ACCIDENT n. An appetizer one finds out has pork

The Definition of Chutzpah

A little old Jewish lady sold pretzels on a street corner for 25 cents each. Every day a young man would leave his office building at lunch time, and as he passed the pretzel stand, he would leave her a quarter, but never take a pretzel.

And this went on for more then 3 years. The two of them never spoke. One day, as the young man passed the old lady's stand and left his quarter as usual, the pretzel lady spoke to him.

"Sir, I appreciate your business. You are a good customer, but I have to tell you that the pretzel price has gone up to 35 cents."

*   *   *   *   *

A Jewish grandma and her grandson are at the beach. He's playing in the water, she is standing on the shore not wanting to get her feet wet, when all of a sudden, a huge wave appears from nowhere and crashes directly onto the spot where the boy is wading. The water recedes and the boy is no longer there.. he was swept away.

The grandma holds her hands to the sky, screams and cries, "Lord, my GOD, how could you? Haven't I been a wonderful grandmother? Haven't I been a wonderful mother? Haven't I kept a kosher home? Haven't I given to charity? Haven't I lit candles every Friday night? Haven't I tried my very best to live a life that you would be proud of?"

A voice booms from the sky, "All right already!"

A moment later another huge wave appears out of nowhere and crashes on the beach. As the water recedes, the boy is standing there. He is smiling and splashing around as if nothing had ever happened.

The voice booms again. "I have returned your grandson. Are you satisfied?"

She responds, "He had a hat."

*   *   *   *   *

The New York City Public Schools have officially declared Jewish English, now dubbed Hebonics, as a second language. Backers of the move say the city schools are the first in the nation to recognize Hebonics as a valid language and a significant attribute of American culture.

According to a linguistics professor at Brooklyn College and renowned Hebonics scholar, the sentence structure of Hebonics derives from middle and eastern European language patterns, as well as Yiddish.

He explains, "In Hebonics, the response to any question is usually another question with a complaint that is either implied or stated. Thus 'How are you?' may be answered, 'How should I be, with my bad feet?' he says that Hebonics is a superb linguistic vehicle for expressing sarcasm or skepticism. An example is the repetition of a word with "sh" or "shm" at the beginning: "Mountains, shmountains. Stay away. You should want a nosebleed?"

Another Hebonics pattern is moving the subject of a sentence to the end, with its pronoun at the beginning: "It's beautiful, that dress."

He says one also sees the Hebonics verb moved to the end of the sentence. Thus the response to a remark such as "He's slow as a turtle," could be: "Turtle, shmurtle! Like a fly in Vaseline he walks."

He provided the following examples:

Question: "What time is it?"
English answer: "Sorry, I don't know."
Hebonic response: "What am I, a clock?"

Remark: "Hurry up. Dinner's ready."
English answer: "Be right there."
Hebonic response: "All right already, I'm coming. What's with the 'hurry' business? Is there a fire?"

Remark: "I like the tie you gave me; I wear it all the time."
English answer: "Glad you like it."
Hebonic response: "So what's the matter; you don't like the other ties I gave you?"

Remark: "Sarah and I are engaged."
English answer: "Congratulations!"
Hebonics response: "She could stand to lose a few pounds."

Question: "Would you like to go riding with us?"
English answer: "Just say when."
Hebonic response: "Riding, schmiding! Do I look like a cowboy?"

To the guest of honor at a birthday party:
English answer: "Happy birthday."
Hebonic response: "A year smarter you should become."

Remark: "A beautiful day."
English answer: "Sure is."
Hebonic response: "So the sun is out; what else is new?"

Answering a phone call from a son:
English answer: "It's been a while since you called."
Hebonic response: "You didn't wonder if I'm dead already?"

Email, shme-mail! Luck and happiness will or will not come to you regardless if you send it to another eight people.

* * * * *

As you know on Rosh Hashanah, there is a ceremony called Tashlich.

7

Jews traditionally go to a body of water such as the ocean, a stream or a river to pray and throw in breadcrumbs. This symbolizes throwing away one's sins which the fish devour. Occasionally, people ask what kinds of breadcrumbs should be thrown. Here are suggestions for breads which may be most appropriate for specific sins and misbehaviors:

For ordinary sins – White Bread

For particularly dark sins – Pumpernickel

For complex sins – Multi grain

For sins of indecision – Waffles

For sins committed in haste – Matzos

For sins of chutzpah – Any fresh bread

For substance abuse/marijuana – Stoned wheat

For substance abuse/heavy drugs – Poppy seed bread

For committing auto theft – Caraway

For timidity/cowardice – Milk toast

For ill-temperedness – Sourdough

For silliness, eccentricity – Nut bread

For excessive irony – Rye bread

For unnecessary chances – Hero bread

For war-mongering – Kaiser rolls

For dressing immodestly – Tarts

For racist attitudes – Crackers

For being holier than thou – Bagels

For overeating – Stuffing

For raising your voice too often – Challah

For pride and egotism – Puff pastry

For the sin of perfectionism – Angel food cake

For trashing the environment – Dumplings

For telling bad jokes/puns – Corn bread

For exotic sins...French bread

For twisted sins...Pretzels

For tasteless sins...Rice cakes

For the sin of committing arson...Toast

For the sin of being money hungry...Raw dough

For the sin of promiscuity...Hot buns

For the sin of promiscuity with Gentiles...Hot cross buns

For the sin of gambling...Fortune cookies

For the sin of abrasiveness...Grits

For negligent slip-ups...Banana bread

For the sin of dropping in without warning...Popovers

For the sin of being up-tight and irritable...High fiber bran muffins

Remember, you don't have to show your crumbs to anyone. For those who require a whole selection of crumbs, an attempt will be made to have pre-packaged Tashlich Mix available in three grades (Tashlich Lite, Regular and Industrial Strength) at your local grocery store.

* * * * *

Shortest fairy tale ever:

Once upon a time a guy asked a Jewish American Princess from Miami Beach, "Will you marry me?" she said, "No" And the guy lived happily ever after!

* * * * *

Seen at Fleegleman's Kosher Deli: The customer is always right; misinformed maybe-perhaps impolite, stubborn and irate, even dumb,… but never wrong.

* * * * *

Q-What is the technical term for a divorced Jewish woman?
A-The plaintiff

* * * * *

Homeless person to a Jewish-American Princess(JAP), "I haven't eaten in three days."

Her reply,"I wish I had your will power."

* * * * *

The Lotus & the Mishpokheh –
The Principles of Jewish Buddhism

If there is no self, whose arthritis is this?

Be here now.
Be someplace else later.
Is that so complicated?

Drink tea and nourish life;
With the first sip, joy;
With the second sip, satisfaction;
With the third, peace;
With the fourth, a Danish.

Wherever you go, there you are.
Your luggage is another story.

Accept misfortune as a blessing.
Do not wish for perfect health, or a life without problems.
What would you talk about?

There is no escaping karma.
In a previous life,
You never called,
You never wrote,
You never visited.
And whose fault was that?

Zen is not easy.
It takes effort to attain nothingness.
And then what do you have?

Bupkis.

The Tao does not blame.
The Tao does not take sides.
The Tao has no expectations.
The Tao demands nothing of others.
The Tao is not Jewish.

Breathe in.
Breathe out.
Breathe in.
Breathe out.
Forget this, and attaining Enlightenment will be the least of your problems.

Let your mind be as a floating cloud.
Let your stillness be as a wooden glen.
And sit up straight.
You'll never meet the Buddha with such rounded shoulders.

Deep inside you are ten thousand flowers.
Each flower blossoms ten thousand times.
Each blossom has ten thousand petals.
You might want to see a specialist.

Be aware of your body.
Be aware of your perceptions.
Keep in mind that not every physical sensation is a symptom of a terminal illness.

The Torah says,
Love your neighbor as yourself.
The Buddha says,
There is no self.
So, maybe we're off the hook?

The Buddha taught that one should practice loving kindness to all beings.
Still, would it kill you to find a nice sentient being who happens to be Jewish?

Jewish Haikus

After the warm rain
The sweet smell of camellias.
Did you wipe your feet?

Her lips near my ear,
Aunt Sadie whispers the name
Of her friend's disease.

Looking for pink buds
To prune, the old moyel
Wanders among his flowers.

Harsh Scrabble discord—
Someone has placed "putzhead" on
A triple word score.

Testing the warm milk on her wrist, she sighs softly.
But her son is forty.

Tea ceremony—
Fragrant steam perfumes the air.
Try the cheese Danish.

A cat steals into
The night just like my former
Partner, that gonif.

Hey! Get back indoors.
Whatever you were doing
Could put an eye out.

Hidden connection –
Starvation in Africa,
Food left on my plate.

How soft the petals
of the floral arrangement
I have just stolen.

My nature journal –
Today, I saw some trees and birds.
I should know the names?

Like a bonsai tree,
Your terrible posture at
My dinner table.

Coroner's report –
"The deceased, wearing no hat,
Caught his death of cold."

The sparrow brings home
Too many worms for her young.
"Force yourself," she chirps.

The shivah visit:
So sorry about your loss.
Now back to my problems.

Our youngest daughter,
Our most precious jewel.
Hence the name, Tiffany.

Mom, please! There is no
Need to put that dinner roll
In your pocketbook.

Seven-foot Jews in
The NBA slam-dunking!
My alarm clock rings.

Sorry I'm not home
To take your call. At the tone
Please state your bad news.

Left the door open.
For the Prophet Elijah.
Now our cat is gone.

Hard to tell under
The lights—white yarmulke or
Male-pattern baldness?

A modern Orthodox Jewish couple, preparing for a religious wedding meets with their Rabbi for counseling. The rabbi asks if they have any last questions before they leave.

The man asks, "Rabbi, we realize it's tradition for men to dance with men, and women to dance with women at the reception. But, we'd like your permission to dance together, like the rest of the world."

"Absolutely not," says the Rabbi. "It's immodest. Men and women always dance separately."

"So after the ceremony I can't even dance with my own wife?" "No," answered the Rabbi. "It's forbidden."

"Well, okay," says the man, "What about sex? Can we finally have sex?"

"Of course!," replies the Rabbi. "Sex is a mitzvah – a good thing within marriage, to have children!"

"What about different positions?" asks the man.

"No problem," says the Rabbi. "It's a mitzvah!"

"Woman on top?" the man asks.

"Sure," says the Rabbi. "Go for it! It's a mitzvah!"

"Doggy style?"

"Sure! Another mitzvah!"

"On the kitchen table?"

"Yes, yes! A mitzvah!"

"Can we do it on rubber sheets with a bottle of hot oil, a couple of vibrators, a leather harness, a bucket of honey and a porno video?"

"You may indeed. It's all a mitzvah!"

"Can we do it standing up?"

"No." says the Rabbi."

"Why not?" asks the man.

"Could lead to dancing."

Lessons You Learn Growing Up Jewish

Number One:

THE PURPOSE OF RELATIVES IS FOR YOU TO BE COMPARED UNFAVORABLY TO THEM

"Do you realize that you are thirteen years old and have wasted the entire day playing that idiotic video game? Do you know that by the time your Uncle Arthur was nine, he was already supporting his family with two jobs, plus going to school and taking care of three sick birds and his paraplegic cousin Rivka?"

"Don't be smart with me, young man. Your asthmatic brother Steven, bless his heart, never opens his mouth to his parents; he knows respect, you should take a lesson."

"If your Grandpa Morris was alive to see how you behave, it would kill him. Now there's a man who knew the meaning of suffering and sacrifice. I never told you this, but he once fell off a ladder, fractured his hip, and still finished out the work week, because he knew his family wouldn't eat if he didn't bring home a paycheck. Are you listening to me?"

Number Two:

BEHIND EVERY POSSIBLE FUN ACTIVITY LURKS THE PROSPECT OF SICKNESS, DISEASE, INJURY, OR DEATH

"I don't want you eating sushi; that's Goyishe food. It is not just like eating lox, lox is smoked."

If you insist on bringing sushi home, at least cook the fish first. You have no idea what kinds of tapeworms and parasites you could be letting yourself in for.

"Next thing you know, you'll be trying to go swimming without waiting half an hour after eating."

"Your great-uncle Mort almost drowned that way. And if you're at the beach, be sure to wear plenty of sunblock plus a t-shirt, and it wouldn't kill you to sit under a beach umbrella, with sunglasses and a hat."

"Sex? Don't even get me started on sex. There's AIDS, social diseases, who knows what kind of jungle rot that could give you? Your uncle Phil nearly died. He had to have his schmeckle amputated after dating some infected shicksa."

"No, I don't mind if you go to the party. Just don't drink anything. They spike the punch, you know. Then I'll get a call that you've wrapped the Camry around a tree. And don't have any of the food, either. You never know."

"Okay, sweetheart. Goodbye. I love you. Have fun. Be home by ten."

Number Three:

YOUR HUNGER LEVEL IS DETERMINED BY THE MISFORTUNES OF CHILDREN IN OTHER COUNTRIES

"Can't finish your brisket? Better eat it all; children are starving in China." I'd offer to send the remainder of my brisket to the starving Chinese children. My mother responded that that's not funny. I agreed with her. I was serious.

It wasn't hard to envision Federal Express planes carrying tons of ungrateful Jewish children's leftover brisket to Shanghai. Perhaps I could even include a note:

"Dear Chun Lee, please enjoy my leftover brisket, courtesy of my mother, Shirley, who assures me that you will appreciate it far more than some spoiled rotten Jewish children who have no idea how good they have it and would thank their lucky stars they're living in America if they spent even one day in some Third World country where you couldn't even find a box of matzoh if your life depended on it. You might want to heat it up a little first. And by the way, next month you can look forward to some nice chopped liver, made from unappreciated liver and onions."

Number Four:

GOOD FURNITURE LASTS MUCH LONGER IF YOU NEVER USE IT

"Why do we keep plastic covers on the couch and chairs? Because they're for company only, not for daily use. If you have to sit during non-company times, choose another couch or chair."

"Why? Oh, I don't know – maybe it's because we don't want dog and grape jelly stains all over our fine furniture for our guests, after your father has worked his fingers to the bone earning the money so we'll have a nice home, not that you've noticed. Maybe we don't want springs and stuffing to be poking through. Maybe we'd like to have at least one room in this house that doesn't look like Arnold Schwarzenegger had a riot in it. Maybe we'd like to have one piece of furniture that our pets and kids don't cause to disintegrate. If that makes us mean or weird or unfair, so be it. Now, get off the couch. And go wash up. I made brisket."

Jewish Rules...

1. Never take a front-row seat at a bris.

2. If you can't say something nice, say it in Yiddish.

3. The High Holidays have nothing to do with marijuana.

4. And what's wrong with dry turkey?

5. A good kugle sinks in mercury.

6. Pork is forbidden, but a pig in a blanket makes a nice hors d'oeuvre.

7. Always whisper the names of diseases.

8. One mitzvah can change the world; two will just make you tired.

9. Never leave a restaurant empty-handed.

10. The important Jewish holidays are the ones on which alternate-side-of-the-street parking is suspended.

11. A bad matzo ball makes a good paperweight.

12. Without Jewish mothers, who would need therapy?

13. According to Jewish dietary law, pork and shellfish may be eaten only in Chinese restaurants.

14. If you are going to whisper at the movies, make sure it's loud enough for everyone else to hear.

15. No meal is complete without leftovers.

16. If you have to ask the price, you can't afford it. But if you can, make sure you tell everybody what you paid.

17. The only good thing more important than a good education is a good parking spot at the mall.

18. It's not whom you know, it's whom you know that had a nose job.

19. After the destruction of the Second Temple, God created Loehmann's.

20. WASPs leave and never say good-bye. Jews say good-bye and never leave.

21. Israel is the land of milk and honey; Florida is the land of milk of magnesia.

22. If you don't eat it, it will kill me.

23. Anything worth saying is worth repeating a thousand times.

24. Next year in Jerusalem. The year after, how about a nice cruise?

25. Spring ahead, fall back, winter in Miami.

26. Laugh now, but one day you'll be driving a big Cadillac and eating dinner at four in the afternoon.

27. It's not really a Jewish holiday if it isn't about eating or not eating.

28. No matter what, you are never good enough for her daughter unless you are a doctor, and you will never be good enough for her son.

29. Never pass up a chance to say "if only."

AND LAST, BUT CERTAINLY NOT LEAST:

30. There comes a time in every man's life when he must stand up and tell his mother that he is an adult. This usually happens at around age 45.

A Hassidic family is most concerned that their 30-year-old son is unmarried.

So they call a marriage broker and ask her to find their son a good wife.

The broker comes over to their house and spends a long time asking many questions of the son and his parents as to what they want in a wife/daughter-in-law.

They give her a long shopping list of requirements.

The marriage broker takes a long time looking and finally asks to visit the family again. She tells them of a wonderful woman she has found. She says she's just the right age for the son…she keeps a kosher home…she regularly attends prayers…she is a wonderful cook…she loves children and wants a large family and, to crown it all off, she's gorgeous.

After hearing all this, the family is very impressed and begins to get excited about the prospects of a wedding in the near future.

But the son pauses and asks, "Is she also good in bed?"

The marriage broker answers, "Some say yes…some say no."

* * * * *

A dietitian is addressing an audience in the Shalom Retirement Home.

"The material we put into our stomachs is enough to have killed most of us sitting here years ago."

"Red meat is awful. Soft drinks erode your stomach lining."

"Chinese food is loaded with MSG. Vegetables can be dirty and disastrous, and none of us realizes the long-term harm caused by the germs in our drinking water."

"But there is one thing that is the most dangerous of all and most of us have eaten it. Can anyone here tell me what food it is that causes the most grief and suffering for years after you eat it?"

In the front row, 75-year-old Morris stands up and says, "Wedding cake!"

* * * * *

Three Texans are sitting together on an airplane. Two are hardy, tall men wearing cowboy boots and 10 gallon hats. The third is a little old Jewish man wearing a yarmulke, short pants, and high black sox with sandles.

The first Texans says: My name is Roger, I have 2000 acres and 3,000 head of cattle. I call my place "The Jolly Roger."

The second Texan says, "My name is Gene. I own 5000 acres and 5000 cattle. I call my place "Gene's Ranch estate."

The little old Jewish man says: "I own 200 acres, and got no cattle."

"And what do you call your place?" says Roger sarcastically.

"Downtown Dallas," says the old Jewish man.

* * * * *

This Black comes into an auto showroom and asks to see a 2007 Cadillac convertible. The salesman tries to steer him to a Chevy, then a Buick, but the customer is adamant and wants to see a brand new Caddy.

The salesman takes him over to the brand new Caddy, the Black gets in, sits down and starts playing with all the buttons, but he keeps looking at his image in the rear view mirror.

The salesman asks if anything is wrong, and is answered, "Do you think I look too much like a Jew in this car?"

(Just a quick note: The first time I heard that story it was a 1952 Caddy El Dorado.)

*   *   *   *   *

A man goes to the eye doctor. The receptionist asks him why he is there.

The man complains, "I keep seeing spots in front of my eyes."

The receptionist asks, "Have you ever seen a doctor?"

And the man replies, "No, just spots."

*   *   *   *   *

A couple had been married for 50 years. They were sitting at the breakfast table one morning when the wife says, "Just think, fifty years ago we were sitting here at this breakfast table together."

"I know," the old man said, "We were probably sitting here naked as jaybirds fifty years ago."

"Well," Granny snickered, "Let's relive some old times."

Whereupon the two stripped to the buff and sat down at the table.

"You know, honey," the little old lady breathlessly replied, "My nipples are as hot for you today as they were fifty years ago."

"I wouldn't be surprised," replied Gramps. "One's in your coffee and the other is in your oatmeal."

*   *   *   *   *

A group of Americans were traveling by tour bus through Holland. As they stopped at a cheese farm, a young guide led them through the process of cheese making, explaining that goat's milk was used. She showed the group a lively hillside where many goats were grazing.

"These" she explained "are the older goats, put out to pasture when they no longer produce." She then asked, "What do you do in America with your old goats?"

A spry old gentleman answered, "They send us on tours, and let us live in Florida and Arizona."

* * * * *

These are actual Personal Ads from Israeli newspapers:

I take out the Torah Saturday morning.
Would like to take you out Saturday night.

Couch potato latke in search of the right applesauce.
Let's try it for 8 days.
Who knows?

Divorced Jewish man seeks partner to attend shul, light shabbos candles, celebrate holidays, build Sukkah together, attend brisses, bar mitzvahs – Religion not important.

Orthodox woman with get, seeks man who got get or can get get.
Get it?
I'll show you mine
If you show me yours.

Sincere rabbinical student, 27, enjoys Yom Kippur, Tisha B'av, Taanis Esther, Tzom Gedalia, Asarah B'Teves, Shiva Asar b'Tammuz.
Seeks companion for living life in the "fast" lane.

Yeshiva bochur, Torah scholar, long beard, payes.
Seeks same in woman.

Nice Jewish guy, 38.
No skeletons.
No baggage.
No personality.

Female graduate student, studying kaballah, Zohar, exorcism of
dybbuks,
Seeks mensch.
No weirdos, please.

Jewish businessman, 49, manufactures Sabbath candles, Chanukah
candles, Havdallah candles, Yahrzeit candles.
Seeks non-smoker.

I am a sensitive Jewish prince whom you can open your heart to, share
your innermost thoughts and deepest secrets. Confide in me. I'll
understand your insecurities.
No fatties, please

Jewish male, 34, very successful, smart, independent, self-made, looking
for girl whose father will hire me.

Final New Year Greeting For The Year!

You must remember this,
A bris is still a bris,
A chai is just a chai.
Pastrami still belongs on rye,
As time goes by.

With holidays in view,
A Jew is still a Jew,
On that you can rely.
No matter if we eat tofu
As hours slip by.

Old shtetl customs, never out of date.
All those potatoes mother has to grate.
Honey, tsimus, latkes, chopped liver on our plate
The best that gelt can buy.

Some would send us to perdition,
But we're strengthened by tradition,
That no one can deny.
We roam, but we recall our birthright,
As time goes by.

Dreidels and chocolate, never out of date.
Ancient Jewish stories to which we all relate.
Blue-and-white giftwrap, everything that's great?
And festive chazerai!

It's still the same old Torah,
It's still the same menorah,
We've latkes still to fry.
It's at yomtov when we fell most blessed,
As time goes by.

Synagogue Seating Request Form For Yom Kippur

During the last holiday season, many individuals expressed concern over the seating arrangements in the synagogue. In order for us to place you in a seat which will best suit you, we ask you to complete the following questionnaire and return it to the synagogue office as soon as possible.

1. I would prefer to sit in the... (Check one)
_____ Talking section
_____ No talking section

2. If talking, which category do you prefer?
(Indicate order of interest)
_____ Stock market
_____ Sports
_____ Medicine
_____ General gossip
_____ Specific gossip (choose)
_____ The Rabbi
_____ The Cantor
_____ The Cantor's voice
_____ The Cantor's significant other
_____ The Rabbi's wife or husband
_____ Fashion news
_____ What others are wearing
_____ Why they look awful
_____ Your neighbors
_____ Your relatives
_____ Your neighbor's relatives
_____ Presidential Election (uh oh)
_____ Sex (Preference): _____
_____ Who's cheating on/having an affair with whom
_____ Other: _____

3. Which of the following would you like to be near for free professional advice?

_____ Doctor
_____ Dentist
_____ Nutritionist
_____ Psychiatrist
_____ Child Psychiatrist
_____ Podiatrist
_____ Chiropractor
_____ Stockbroker
_____ Accountant
_____ Lawyer
_____ Criminal
_____ Civil
_____ Real estate agent
_____ Architect
_____ Plumber
_____ Buyer (Specify store: _____)
_____ Sexologist
_____ Golf pro [tentative; we're still trying to find a Jewish One]
_____ Other: _____

4. I want a seat located (indicate order of priority)

_____ On the aisle
_____ Near the exit
_____ Near the window
_____ In Aruba
_____ Near the bathroom
_____ Near my in-laws
_____ As far away from my in-laws as possible
_____ As far away from my ex-in-laws as possible
_____ Near the pulpit
_____ Near the Kiddush table
_____ Near single men
_____ Near available women
_____ Where no one on the bimah can see/hear me talking during services

_____ Where no one will notice me sleeping during services
_____ Where I can sleep during the Rabbi's sermon [additional charge]

5. (Orthodox only.) I would like a seat where:
_____ I can see my spouse over the mechitza
_____ I cannot see my spouse over the mechitza
_____ I can see my friend's spouse over the mechitza
_____ my spouse cannot see me looking at my friend's spouse over the mechitza

6. Please do not place me anywhere near the following people:
(Limit of six; if you require more space, you may wish to consider joining another congregation.)

_____

_____

_____

_____

_____

_____

Your name: _____
Building fund pledge: $_____

A man goes to a doctor for a complete physical check-up because he hasn't been feeling well.

After the check-up the doctor comes out with the results of the examination.

"I'm afraid I have some bad news, you're dying and don't have much time," the doctor says.

"Oh no, that's terrible. How long have I got?" the man asks.

"Ten......" says the doctor.

"Ten? Ten what. Months? Weeks? What?!"

"Ten, nine, eight, seven....."

* * * * *

An elderly gentleman went to the local drug store and asked the pharmacist to fill his prescription for Viagra. "How many do you want?" asked the pharmacist.

The man replied, "Just a few, maybe half a dozen. I cut each one into four pieces."

Upon hearing that, the pharmacist said, "that's too small a dose. That won't get you through sex."

The old fellow said, "Oh, I'm past ninety years old and I don't even think about sex anymore. I just want it to stick out enough so I don't pee on my shoes."

Learn Chinese in Five (5) minutes

(You MUST read them out loud.)

English	Chinese
That's not right	Sum Ting Wong
Are you harboring a fugitive?	Hu Yu Hai Ding
See me ASAP	Kum Hia Nao
Small horse	Tai Ni Po Ni
Did you go to the beach?	Wai Yu So Tan
I think you need a face lift	Chin Tu Fat
It's very dark in here	Wai So Dim
I thought you were on a diet	Wai Yu Mun Ching
This is a tow away zone	No Pah King
Our meeting is scheduled for next week	Wai Yu Kum Nao
Staying out of sight	Lei Ying Lo
He's cleaning his automobile	Wa Shing Ka
Your body odor is offensive	Yu Stin Ki Pu

Advice From A Rabbi

No matter what this husband did in bed, his wife never achieved an orgasm. Since a Jewish wife is entitled to sexual pleasure, they decide to consult their Rabbi.

The Rabbi listens to their story, strokes his beard, and makes the following suggestion: "Hire a strapping young man. While the two of you are making love, have the young man wave a towel over you. That will help the wife fantasize, and should bring on an orgasm." They go home, and follow the Rabbi's advice. They hire a handsome young man, and he waves a towel over them as they make love. It doesn't help, and the wife is still unsatisfied.

Perplexed, they go back to the Rabbi.

"Okay," he says to the husband, "Try it reversed. Have the young man make love to your wife, and you wave the towel over them." Once again, they follow the Rabbi's advice. They go home, and hire the same strapping young man. The young man gets into bed with the wife, and the husband waves the towel. The young man gets to work with great enthusiasm, and the wife soon has an enormous, room-shaking, ear-splitting, screaming orgasm. The husband smiles, looks at the young man, and says triumphantly:

"You see, you young schmuck? THAT's how you wave a towel.!"

* * * * *

One day at kindergarten a teacher said to the class of 5-year-olds, I'll give $10 to the child who can tell me who was the most famous man who ever lived." An Irish boy put his hand up and said, "It was St. Patrick." The teacher said, "Sorry Sean, that's not correct."

Then a Scottish boy put his hand up and said, "It was St. Andrew."

The teacher replied, "I'm sorry, Hamish, that's not right either."

Finally, a Jewish boy raised his hand and said, "It was Jesus Christ."

The teacher said, "That's absolutely right, Marvin, come up here and I'll give you the $10."

As the teacher was giving Marvin his money, she said, "You know Marvin, since you're Jewish; I was very surprised you said Jesus Christ."

Marvin replied, "Yeah. In my heart I knew it was Moses, but business is business..."

* * * * *

A Jewish mother's answering machine:

If you want lox and eggs, press 1;
If you want knishes press 2;
If you want chicken soup, press 3;
If you want matzoh balls with the soup, press 4;
If you want to know how am I feeling, you are calling THE WRONG NUMBER since NOBODY ever asks me how I am feeling. Who knows I could even be dead by now.

* * * * *

Jack has died. His lawyer is standing before the family and reads out Jack's Last Will and Testament. "To my dear wife Esther, I leave the house, 50 acres of land, and 1 million dollars. To my son Barry, I leave my Big Lexus and the Jaguar. To my daughter Suzy, I leave my yacht and $250,000. And to my brother-in-law Jeff, who always insisted that health is better than wealth, I leave my sun lamp."

* * * * *

Bernie had a fight with Rachel, his wife, and went to the movies to cool off.

Later that evening, he decided to phone home to see what the situation was and maybe even apologize.

"Hello, darling," he said, "what are you making for dinner?"

"What am I making for dinner? After all the horrible things you said to me earlier, you want to know what I am making for dinner?? Poison, that's what I'm making, poison." Bernie replies: "Okay then, just make one portion, I'm not coming home."

* * * * *

Miriam was dying and on her deathbed, she gave final instructions to her husband Sidney.

"Sidney, you've been so good to me all these years. But now that I'm going, I want you to marry again as soon as possible and I want you to give your new wife all my expensive clothes."

"I can't do that, darling," Sidney said. "You're a size 16 and she's only a 10."

* * * * *

A man who has finally made it big in business treats himself to a new Lamborghini. After buying it, he feels guilty so he goes to the Orthodox Rabbi and asks for a mezuzah for the Lamborghini.

"You want a mezuzah for what?" the Rabbi asks.

"It's a Lamborghini."

"What's a Lamborghini?" asks the Rabbi.

"A sports car."

"What? That's blasphemy!" the Rabbi shouts. "You want a mezuzah for a sports car? Go to the Conservatives!"

Well, the man is disappointed, but goes to the Conservative Rabbi and asks for a mezuzah.

"You want a mezuzah for what?" the Rabbi asks.

"It's a Lamborghini.", the man replies.

"What's a Lamborghini?" asks the Rabbi.

"A car, a sports car."

"What? That's blasphemy!" the Rabbi shouts. "You want a mezuzah for a Goyishe car? Go to the Reform!"

Again, the man feels guilty and disappointed, but goes to the Reform Rabbi.

"Rabbi," he asks, "I'd like a mezuzah for my Lamborghini."

"You have a Lamborghini?" asks the Rabbi.

"You know what it is?" says the man.

"Of course! It's a fantastic Italian sports car. What's a mezuzah?"

* * * * *

ANOTHER VERSION

This man is being pressured by his kids to get a Christmas tree, but he just doesn't feel right about it.

He goes to the Orthodox Rabbi in the shul where he grew up and asks him to make a Brucha over the tree. The Rabbi throws him out.

He then goes to a Conservative Rabbi and asks him to make a Brucha over the tree. The Rabbi goes into a long, learned discussion about the pros and cons of assimilation, but say he just can't see his way free to do this.

He then goes to a Reform Rabbi and asks him to make a Brucha over the tree.

The Reform Rabbi agrees, but has one question.

"What's a Brucha?"

* * * * *

A young Jew and an old Jew are riding on a bus in Jerusalem.

The young Jew asks, "Excuse me, sir, what time is it?"

The old Jew doesn't answer.

"Excuse me, sir," the young Jew asks again, "what time is it?"

The old Jew still doesn't answer.

"Sir, forgive me for interrupting you all the time, but I really want to know what time it is. Why won't you answer me?"

The old Jew says, "Son, the next stop is the last on this route. I don't know you, so you must be a stranger. If I answer you now, according to Jewish tradition, I must invite you to my home. You're handsome and I have a beautiful daughter. You will both fall in love and you'll want to get married. And tell me, why would I want a son-in-law who can't even afford a damn watch?"

Chutzpah

… according to the Funk & Wagnall's Standard Desk Dictionary - US slang meaning: brazen, effrontery, nerve, impudence, having gall, cheeky. The word is Hebrew in origin.

Bill Gates decides to organize an enormous session of recruitment for a chairman for Microsoft Europe. The 5000 candidates are all assembled in a large room. One of the candidates is Maurice Cohen, a little Parisian Jewish Tunisian.

Bill Gates thanks all the candidates for coming and asks that all those who do not know JAVA program language rise and leave. 2000 people rise and leave the room. Maurice Cohen says to himself - "I do not know this language but what have I got to lose if I stay? I'll give it a try".

Bill Gates asks all the candidates that those who have never had experience of team management of more than 100 people rise and leave. 2000 people rise and leave the room. Maurice Cohen says to himself - "I have never managed anybody but myself but what have I got to lose if I stay? What can happen to me?" So he stays.

Then Bill Gates asks all the candidates who do not have excellent management diplomas to rise and leave. 500 people rise and leave the room. Maurice Cohen says to himself - "Left school at 15 but what have I got to lose if I stay?" So he stays in the room.

Lastly, Bill Gates asks all of the candidates who do not speak the Serbo-Croat language to rise and leave. 498 people rise and leave the room. Maurice Cohen says to himself - "I do not speak Serbo-Croat but what the hell! - have I got anything to lose?" So he stays in the room. He finds himself alone with one other candidate - everyone else has gone.

Bill Gates joins them and says: "Apparently you are the only two candidates who speak Serbo-Croatian, so I'd now like to hear you both have a little conversation in that language!"

Calmly Maurice turns to the other candidate and says to him: "Baroukh ata Adonai."

The other candidate answers: "Elohenou melekh haolam."

* * * * *

This Martian comes to Earth and is interviewed. He is asked, "Are all Martians short?" and answers, "Yes".

"Are all Martians green in color?" He answers, "Yes".

"Do all Martians wear three gold chains around their necks?".

And he answers, "Only the Jewish Martians".

* * * * *

An elderly Jewish man is standing at an upright urinal in a Public Restroom when a big Black man runs in, heaves a big sigh of relief and starts urinating at the next urinal. He sighs a big sigh and exclaims, "Just made it."

The little old man looks over and says, "Could you make one for me. In white."

The Rabbi's Widow

In a small town in the Old Country, the Rabbi died. His widow, the Rebbetzin, was so disconsolate that the people of the town decided that she ought to get married again. But the town was so small that the only eligible bachelor was the town butcher. The poor Rebbetzin was somewhat dismayed because she had been wed to a scholar, and the butcher had no great formal education. However, she was lonely, so she agreed, and they were married.

After the marriage, Friday came. She went to the mikvah (a Jewish ritual bath to get rid of impurities). Then, she went home to prepare to light the candles.

The butcher leaned over to her and said, "My mother. Hana, told me that after the mikvah and before lighting the candles, it's good to have sex." So they did.

She lit the candles. He leaned over again and said, "My father, Shmuel, told me that after lighting the candles it's good to have sex." So they did.

They went to bed after saying their prayers. When they awoke he said to her, "My grandmother, Rivka, said that before you go to the synagogue it's good to have sex." So they did.

After praying all morning, they came home to rest; and again he whispers in her ear, "My grandfather, Moishe, says after praying it's good to have sex." So they did.

On Sunday she went out to shop for food and met a friend who asked, "So how is the new husband?"

She replied, "Well, he is no scholar; but he comes from a wonderful family."

* * * * *

Two astronauts land on Mars. Their mission: to check whether there is oxygen on the planet.

"Give me the box of matches" says one. "Either it burns and there is oxygen, or nothing happens."

He takes the box, and is ready to strike a match when out of the blue, a Martian appears waving all his arms... "No, no, don't!"

The two guys look at each other, worried. Could there be an unknown explosive gas on Mars? But he takes another match...

And now a crowd of hysterical Martians is coming, all waving their arms: "No, no, don't do that!"

"It looks serious. What are they afraid of? But – we're here for Science, to know if man can breathe on Mars". He strikes a match, which flames up, burns down, and..... nothing happens.

"Why did you want to prevent us from striking a match?"

The leader of the Martians says, "Its Shabbos!!!!!!!!"

The Encyclopedia of Jewish Expressions

Vay iz meer: An expression which closely resembles "Woe is Me", and is cried out by Jewish mothers every 15 minnutes. An anthem of true suffering.

Goyim: People who are Gentile. A polite term for anyone who doesn't love a good bargain or has extra skin on his schmeckel.

Tattalah: An endearing term of love which means "little man". An emasculating term for women to call men, if you think about it. But who has time to think.

Gefilte Fish: A tasty mix of congealed fish parts and transparent slime jelly. The only food it is permissible for Jewish children to refuse. In some families, they may even be allowed to gag, but politely.

Chalyera: A derogatory term which best refers to a female business associate or a mother-in-law. The closest English equivalent is "bitch".

Koorveh: A call-girl, or prostitute. A reference to the Russian Czar's wife at the turn of the 20th Century, and to that flashy shiksa your nephew married. Also known as Nafkeh.

Kugel: A yummy blend of overcooked noodles, raisins, and curds of ripe cheese. Not fun to look at. When lathered with sour cream makes an excellent artery hardener.

Borscht: A purple soup made from beets and ammonia. Often eaten by elderly Ashkenazic Jews who slurp noisily and have protruding nose hair. Which is helpful, because it stinks to high heaven.

K'naidlach: Also referred to as matzoh balls. Made with Styrofoam and sponges. There isn't a laxative in the world strong enough to counteract them.

Schmendrick: A man who messes things up, always loses and feels miserable. Closely related to Schlemazel and Schlemiell. Every Jewish family has at least one.

Schlemiel: A jerk who can't do anything right. In simple terms, someone who's always spilling his soup.

Schlemazel: The poor dumb putz a Schlemiell is always spilling soup on.

Tsuris: A word referring to all problems, trouble, grief, aggravation and heartache. Examples: daughter pregnant with child of an unemployed Catholic bartender, adult son loses job and moves back home.

Major Tsuris: Daughter and baby "Bridget" move back home too.

Latkes: Potato pancakes fried in castor oil and lightly seasoned with balsa wood.? Smells like old boxer shorts.

Ken in-a-hura: A gleeful rejoice used when Jewish parents find out their daughter is going to marry a Jewish doctor.

*　*　*　*　*

Exhausted and overworked, Santa Claus has decided to convert to Judaism to lessen his workload and decrease his stress. Mr. Claus's first inkling that Judaism was his new intended path was when he was unloading one particularly heavy bag of gifts and muttered "Oy Oy Oy" instead of "Ho Ho Ho"

Santa took this as divine inspiration and began some serious reflection on the matter. He sat down at his desk in the North Pole and itemized the benefits of bringing toys to Jewish children.

Most obvious was that therte were much less children to service, approximately 3,000,0000 Jewish children as opposed to almost 500,000,000 Christian children. The next obvious benefit was that he had eight days of Hanukah to deliver all of these gifts instead of jamming the entire shipment into one night, which constantly required the already weary Santa to travel at the speed of light to accomplish the task.

Finally, the straw that broke the reindeer's back was the realization that Jewish households had far more delicious cuisine to offer. Gefilte fish, chicken soup, Kosher hot dogs, bagels and the like are more palatable than the milk and cookies he got bored of after the second century.

Circumcision won't be necessary for Santa, because that's already been taken care of in a freak accident involving frostbite after getting stuck in a tight chimney.

Santa has left the frigid, brutal confines of the North Pole and has begun his toy shop anew in the sunny climes of Boynton Beach, Florida.

He has fired all of those annoying elves and replaced them with nice Jewish retirees from Buffalo, New York.

* * * * *

We give the answer. You give the question.

A: Babylon
Q: What does the Rabbi do during some sermons?

A: The Gaza Strip
Q: What is an Egyptian Belly Dance?

A: A classroom, a Passover ceremony, and a latke
Q: What are a cheder, a seder, and a tater?

A: Shofar
Q: On what do Jews recline on Passover?

A: Filet Minyan
Q: What do you call steaks ordered by 10 Jews?

A: Kishka, sukkah, and circumcision
Q: What are a gut, a hut, and a cut?

And speaking of circumcisions: An enterprising Rabbi is offering circumcisions via the Internet. The service is to be called… "E-MOIL."

* * * * *

If a doctor carries a black bag and a plumber carries a tool box, what does a mohel carry?

A. A bris kit! (Oy Vey!)

* * * * *

A Way of Dealing with Anti-Semitism

On a flight from Atlanta, GA., a middle-aged, well to do woman found herself sitting next to a man wearing a kipa (aka yarmulke).

She called the attendant over to complain about her seating.

"What seems to be the problem Madam?" asked the attendant.

"You've sat me next to a Jew!! I can't possibly sit next to this disgusting person. Find me another seat!"

"Please calm down, Madam." The attendant replied.

"The flight is very full today, but I'll tell you what I'll do. I'll go and check to see if we have any seats available."

The woman shoots a snooty look at the snubbed Jewish man beside her (not to mention many of the surrounding passengers).

A few minutes later the attendant returns. The woman cannot help but look at the people around her with a smug and self satisfied grin.

The flight attendant then says… "Madam, unfortunately, as I suspected, economy is full. I've spoken to the cabin services director, and club is also full. However, we do have one seat in first class."

Before the lady has a chance to respond, the attendant continues… "It is most extraordinary to make this kind of upgrade, however, and I have had to get special permission from the captain. But, given the circumstances, the captain felt that it was outrageous that someone should be forced to sit next to such a person."

Then the flight attendant turned to the Jewish man sitting next to her, and said: "So if you'd like to get your things, sir, I have your seat in first class ready for you…"

At this point, the surrounding passengers stood and gave a standing ovation, while the Jewish man walks up to the front of the plane.

* * * * *

Q: What's the title of a horror film for Jewish women?
A: Debby Does The Dusting / Dishes

Q: In Jewish doctrine, when does a fetus become human?
A: When it wins a place in medical school

Q: What does a Jewish woman do to keep her hands soft and her nails long?
A: Nothing at all

Q: Define "genius"
A: An average student with a Jewish mother

Q: Why did the mohel retire?
A: He just couldn't cut it anymore

Q: If Tarzan and Jane were Jewish, what would Cheetah be?
A: A fur coat

Q: What do you call someone who enjoys work and refuses to retire?
A: A meshuggener

Q: What do you call the nipple on a Jewish wife's breast?
A: The tip of the iceberg

Q: What mechanical device causes the most arousal in a Jewish woman?
A: A Mercedes Benz 500SL convertible

* * * * *

Jewish proverb: "A Jewish wife will forgive and forget, but she'll never forget what she forgave."

* * * * *

One of life's mysteries – how a 2 Ib. box of chocolates can make a Jewish woman gain 5 lbs.

Another of life's mysteries is when a Jewish woman hangs something in her wardrobe for a while and it shrinks two sizes!

* * * * *

Q: What is a Jewish ménage-a-trois
A: Two headaches and a hard-on.

Q: Why did Adam and Eve have a perfect marriage?
A: He didn't have to hear about all the men she could have married, and she didn't have to hear about the way his mother cooked

Q: How does a Jewish wife cheat on her husband?
A: She has a headache with the postman.

Q: What business is a yenta in?
A: Yours.

Q: What is a Jewish nymphomaniac?
A: A wife who does her hair and sleeps with her husband on the same day.

Q: How do Jewish wives get their children ready for supper?
A They put them in the car.

Q: What does a Jewish husband call a water bed?
A: The Dead Sea

Q: What is Israel's favorite Internet provider?
A: Netanyahoo

Q: What's the name of the face lotion made especially for Jewish women?
A: Oil of Oy Vay

Q: What is the plural of yenta
A: Hadassah

*   *   *   *   *

Morris returns from a long business trip and finds out that his wife has been unfaithful during his time away.

"Who was it!!!???" he yells. "That idiot Goldstein?"

"No," replied his wife. "It wasn't Goldstein."

"Was it Feldman, that dirty old man?"

"No, not him."

"Aha! Then it must have been that idiot Rabinovich!"

"No, it wasn't Rabinovich either..."

Morris was now fuming. "What's the matter?" he cried. "None of my friends are good enough for you?"

*   *   *   *   *

A couple just started their Lamaze class and they were given an activity requiring the husband to wear a bag of sand to give him an idea of what it feels like to be pregnant. The husband stood up and shrugged saying, "This doesn't feel so bad."

The instructor then dropped a pen and asked the husband to pick it up.

"You want me to pick up the pen as if I were pregnant, the way my wife would do it?" the husband asked.

"Exactly," replied the instructor.

To the delight of the other husbands, he turned to his wife and said, "Honey, pick up that pen for me."

Use of Yiddish in Federal Court in the USA

In the heat of litigation, tempers often flare and lawyers sometimes have difficulty expressing their frustrations. When English fails, Yiddish may come to the rescue. So it happened that defense attorneys arguing in a recent summary judgment motion in federal court in Boston wrote, in a responsive pleading, "It is unfortunate that this Court must wade through the dreck of plaintiff's original and supplemental statement of undisputed facts."

Plaintiffs' attorneys, not to be outdone, responded with a motion that could double as a primer on practical Yiddish for lawyers:

UNITED STATES DISTRICT COURT DISTRICT OF MASSACHUSETTS

MONICA SANTIAGO, Plaintiff, v. SHERWIN-WILLIAMS COMPANY, et al., Defendants.
Civ. No. 87-2799-T

PLAINTIFF'S MOTION TO STRIKE IMPERTINENT AND SCANDALOUS MATTER

Plaintiff, by her attorneys, hereby moves this Court pursuant to Rule 12(f) of the Federal Rules of Civil Procedure to strike as impertinent and scandalous the characterization of her factual submission as "dreck" on page 11 of Defendant's Rule 56.1 Supplemental Statement of Disputed Facts (a copy of which is attached hereto as Exhibit A).

As grounds therefore, plaintiff states:

For almost four years now, plaintiff and her attorneys have been subjected to the constant kvetching by defendants' counsel, who have made a big tsimmes about the quantity and quality of plaintiff's responses to discovery requests. This has been the source of much tsoris among plaintiff's counsel and a gonsa megillah for the Court.

Now that plaintiff's counsel has, after much time and effort, provided defendants with a specific and comprehensive statement of plaintiff's claims and the factual basis thereof, defendants' counsel have the chutzpah to call it "dreck" and to urge the Court to ignore it.

Plaintiff moves that this language be stricken for several reasons.

First, we think it is impertinent to refer to the work of a fellow member of the bar of this Court with the Yiddish term "dreck" as it would be to use "the sibilant four-letter English word for excrement."

Second, defendants are in no position to deprecate plaintiff's counsel in view of the chozzerai which they have filed over the course of this litigation. Finally, since not all of plaintiff's lawyers are yeshiva bochurs defendants should not have assumed that they would all be conversant in Yiddish.

WHEREFORE, plaintiff prays that the Court put an end to the mishagass.

* * * * *

Personal ads from New York Jewish Paper:

Worried about in-law meddling? I'm an orphan!

Staunch Jewish feminist, wears tzitzis, seeking male who will accept my independence, although you probably will not. Oh, just forget it.

Israeli professor, 41, with 18 years of teaching in my behind. Looking for American-born woman who speaks English very good.

80-year-old bubby, no assets, seeks handsome, virile Jewish male, under 35. Object matrimony. I can dream, can't I?

Single Jewish woman, 29, into disco, mountain climbing, skiing, track and field. Has slight limp.

Desperately seeking shmoozing! Retired senior citizen desires female companion 70+ for kvetching, kvelling, krechtzing. Under 30 is also OK.

You may remember the old Jewish Catskill comics from vaudeville days? Here are some of their famous comedy lines. You've probably heard them all before, but don't you miss that kind of humor without using a single swear word in the content?

I've been in love with the same woman for 49 years. If my wife ever finds out, she'll kill me!

What are three words a woman never wants to hear when she's making love? "Honey, I'm home!"

Someone stole all my credit cards, but I won't be reporting it. The thief spends less than my wife did.

We always hold hands. If I let go, she shops.

My wife and I went back to the hotel where we spent our wedding night, only this time, I stayed in the bathroom and cried.

She was at the beauty shop for two hours. That was only for the estimate. She got a mudpack and looked great for two days. Then the mud fell off.

I was just in London – there is a 6-hour time difference. I'm still confused. When I go to dinner, I feel sexy. When I go to bed, I feel hungry.

The doctor gave a man six months to live. The man couldn't pay his bill, so he gave him another six months.

The Doctor called Mrs. Cohen saying, "Mrs. Cohen, your check came back." Mrs. Cohen answered "So did my arthritis!"

The Doctor says, "you'll live to be 60!" "I AM 60!"

"See, what did I tell you?"

A doctor has a stethoscope up to a man's chest. The man asks, "Doc, how do I stand?"

The doctor says, "That's what puzzles me!"

Doctor says to a man, "You're pregnant!" The man says, "how does a man get pregnant?" the doctor says, "The usual way, a little wine, a little dinner…"

"Doctor, I have a ringing in my ears."

"Don't answer!"

A drunk was in front of a judge. The judge says, "You've been brought here for drinking." The drunk says "Okay, let's get started."

A bum asked me, "Give me $10 till payday." I asked "When's payday?" He said "I don't know, you're the one who is working!"

There was a girl knocking on my hotel room door all night! Finally, I let her out.

Q.   Why do Jewish divorces cost so much?
A.   They're worth it.

Q.   Why do Jewish men die before their wives?
A.   They want to.

A car hit a Jewish man. The paramedic says, "Are you comfortable?" the man says, "I make a good living."

I just got back from a pleasure trip. I took my mother-in-law to the airport.

I wish my brother would learn a trade, so I would know what kind of work he's out of.

* * * * *

A judge is ready to go through the day's business and he is very rushed.

The first case up involves an elderly Jewish gentleman with a long beard, payes, ... the works.

The judge, without asking a question, says to the clerk, "Get me a translator."

Translator shows up and the judge says, "Ask him what his name is, how old is he and where does he come from?"

The translator says, "Die judge vilt vissen, vos is ihre namen, vie alt zent ihr, and fun vie kimt ihr?"

The old man smiles, looks at the judge and says in perfect English with a British accent, "Sir. My name is Chiam Ginsburg. I shall be 82 next Thursday and I've come from England where I hold the chair of Hebrew Philosophy at Oxford University."

The translator turns to the judge and says,

"Er zakt, er is Chiam Ginsburg, er is tzwei und achtzig yur alt, und er is, mit sach Yiddish philisoph, areingekummen fun Oxford

* * * * *

A young Jewish man excitedly tells his mother he's fallen in love and going to get married.

He says, "Just for fun, Ma, I'm going to bring over three women and you try and guess which one I'm going to marry." The mother agrees.

The next day, he brings three beautiful women into the house and sits them down on the couch and they chat for a while. He then says, "Okay, Ma. Guess which one I'm going to marry."

She immediately replies, "The red-head in the middle."

"That's amazing, Ma. You're right. How did you know?"

"I don't like her."

* * * * *

Horowitz was feeling ill at work, and left after lunch to go home. He walked into the house and found his wife Fanny in the arms of another man. He started to yell at the interloper, "What right have you got to be making love to my wife?"

The man answered calmly, "You may as well know that I am in love with Fanny and I would like to marry her. I understand you're a gambler. Why don't you be a good sport and sit down and play a game of gin rummy with me? If I lose, I'll never see her again; if you lose, you must agree to divorce her.... Okay?"

"Okay," replied Horowitz, "But just to make it a little more interesting, why don't we play for a dollar a point?"

Jewish Mother's Wisdom

1. My mother taught me TO APPRECIATE A JOB WELL DONE. "If you're going to kill each other, do it outside. I just finished cleaning."

2. My mother taught me RELIGION. "You better pray that will come out of the carpet."

3. My mother taught me about TIME TRAVEL. "If you don't straighten up, I'm going to knock you into the middle of next week!"

4. My mother taught me LOGIC. "Because I said so, that's why."

5. My mother taught me MORE LOGIC. "If you fall out of that swing and break your neck, you're not going to the store with me."

6. My mother taught me FORESIGHT. "Make sure you wear clean underwear, in case you're in an accident."

7. My mother taught me IRONY. "Keep crying, and I'll give you something to cry about."

8. My mother taught me about the science of OSMOSIS. "Shut your mouth and eat your supper."

9. My mother taught me about CONTORTIONISM. "Will you look at that dirt on the back of your neck!"

10. My mother taught me about STAMINA. "You'll sit there until all that spinach is gone."

11. My mother taught me about WEATHER. "This room of yours looks as if a tornado went through it."

12. My mother taught me about HYPOCRISY. "If I told you once, I've told you a million times. Don't exaggerate!"

13. My mother taught me the CIRCLE OF LIFE. "I brought you into this world, and I can take you out."

14. My mother taught me about BEHAVIOR MODIFICATION. "Stop acting like your father!"

15. My mother taught me about ENVY. "There are millions of less fortunate children in this world who don't have wonderful parents like you do."

16. My mother taught me about ANTICIPATION. "Just wait until we get home."

17. My mother taught me about RECEIVING. "You are going to get it when you get home!"

18. My mother taught me MEDICAL SCIENCE. "If you don't stop crossing your eyes, they are going to freeze that way."

19. My mother taught me ESP. "Put your sweater on; don't you think I know when you are cold?"

The Israeli Ambassador at the U.N. began, "Ladies and gentlemen before I commence with my speech, I want to relay an old Passover story to all of you …

"When Moses was leading the Jews out of Egypt toward the Promised Land, he had to go through the nearly endless Sinai desert.

When they reached the Promised Land, the people had became very thirsty and needed water.

So Moses struck the side of a mountain with his staff and a pond appeared with crystal clean, cool water. The people rejoiced and drank to their hearts' content.

"Moses wished to cleanse his whole body, so he went over to the other side of the pond, took all of his clothes off and dived into the cool waters. The only problem was when Moses came out of the water, he discovered that all his clothes had been stolen. 'And,' he said, 'I have reason to believe that the Palestinians stole my clothes.'"

The Palestinian delegate to the UN, hearing this accusation, jumps from his seat and screams out, "This is a travesty. It is widely known that there were no Palestinians there at that time!"

"And with that in mind," said the Israeli Ambassador, "let me now begin my speech."

*   *   *   *   *

A New York judge is presiding over the divorce proceedings of a Jewish couple. When the final papers have been signed and the divorce is complete the woman thanks the judge and says "Now I have to arrange for a Get."

The judge inquires what she means by a Get. So, the woman explains that a Get is a religious ceremony required under the Jewish religion in order to receive a divorce recognized by the Jewish faith.

The judge says, "You mean a religious ceremony like a Bris?"

She replies. "Yes, very similar, only in this case you get rid of the entire schmuck!"

* * * * *

A lady dining in a fine restaurant is about to take a bite when she turns to the man at the table next to her. "Pardon me, sir" she says, "Your napkin has fallen on the floor."

"Oy! Tanks for dat. Vitout you, I vouldn't know. I'm blindt." He reaches down to find his napkin. Once it's back on his lap, he asks her if he has spilled any food on his shirt. "Hardly at all," she answers, "just a few cracker crumbs." "Tanks, again, Missus," he replies, brushing them off. "Vitout you telling, I vouldn't know dese tings." A few moments later, he inquires again, "Do you mind I should ask a poisonal qvestion?" "Not at all," she replies. "I don't do vell vit the ladies. Do you tink I'm ugly?" "You're quite presentable," she replies. "That shouldn't be a problem." Smiling now, he exults, "Vat a relief. I vas alvays afraid to ask. Again, I got to tank you." A few more moments pass and the lady speaks up. "Do you mind if I give you a bit of advice?" she asks. "Soitenly! Listen, I vill take all de help vat you got," he answers. "Lose the Yiddish accent." she replies. "You're a Shvartsa."

* * * * *

A man goes to see the Rabbi. "Rabbi, something terrible is happening and I have to talk to you about it." The Rabbi asked, "What's wrong?" "My wife is poisoning me." The Rabbi, very surprised by this, asks, "Are you sure? Why would she do such a thing?" The man then pleads, "I don't know why, but I'm telling you, I'm certain she's poisoning me. What should I do?"

The Rabbi thinks a bit, then says, "Tell you what. Let me talk to her, I'll see what I can find out and I'll let you know."

A week later the Rabbi calls the man and says, "Well, I spoke with your wife. I called her and we talked on the phone for 3 hours. You want my advice?" The man said yes, and the Rabbi replied, "Take the poison."

*　*　*　*　*

A man arrives at the Ben Gurion International Airport in Tel Aviv with two large bags. The customs agent opens the first bag and finds it full with money in different currencies. The agent asks the passenger, "How did you get this money?" The man says, "You will not believe it, but I traveled all over Europe, went into public restrooms, each time I saw a man pee, I grabbed his penis and said, "donate money to Israel or I will cut your balls off." The customs agent said "Well... it's very interesting story... what do you have in the other bag?" The man said, "You would not believe how many people in Europe do not support Israel".

*　*　*　*　*

Rifka and Beckie are talking about their children. Rifka asks Beckie how her daughter is.

Beckie says, "Not too good. My daughter just divorced her husband. He was a doctor."

Rifka replies "Oh, I am so sorry to hear that."

Beckie continues, "Yes, it is sad. Her first husband, whom she divorced three years ago, was a dentist. But she is OK now, she is dating a handsome lawyer."

Rifka replies, "A dentist, a doctor and a lawyer. All this naches from just one daughter!"

*　*　*　*　*

A little girl became restless as the Rabbi's sermon dragged on and on. Finally, she leaned over to her mother and whispered, "Mommy, if we give him the money now, will he let us go?"

* * * * *

This older Jewish man was on the operating table awaiting surgery and he insisted that his son, a renowned surgeon, perform the operation. As he was about to receive the anesthesia he asked to speak to his son.

"Yes Dad, what is it?"

"Don't be nervous, son, do your best and just remember, if it doesn't go well, if something happens to me ... your mother is going to come and live with you and your wife!"

* * * * *

This Hasidic Jew walks into a bar in Manhattan with a big green frog on his shoulder.

The bartender says, "Where did you get that?"

The frog says, "In Brooklyn, there are hundreds of them there."

* * * * *

Sol visits Abe and sees a dog in the house.

"So what kind of dog is this?" asks Sol.

"It's a Jewish dog." says Abe. "Watch this," continues Abe as he points to the dog. "Fetch!"

Irving walks slowly to the door, then turns around and says, "So why are you talking to me like that? You always order me around like I'm nothing. And then you make me sleep on the floor, with my arthritis... You give me this fahkahkta food with all the salt and fat, and you tell me it's a special diet... It tastes like dreck! YOU should eat it yourself!... And do you ever take me for a decent walk? NO, it's out of the house, a short piss, and right back home. Maybe if I could stretch out a little, the sciatica wouldn't kill me so much!"

Sol, amazed, tells Abe how remarkable this is, to which Abe answers, "I don't know, I think he has a hearing problem. I said fetch, and he thought I said kvetch."

* * * * *

A small town had three shuls - Orthodox, Conservative and Reform. All three had a serious problem with squirrels in their buildings. Each congregation, in its own fashion, had a meeting to deal with the problem.

The Orthodox decided that it was predestined that squirrels be in the Shul and that they would just have to live with them.

The Conservatives decided they should deal with the squirrels in the movement's style of Community Responsibility & Social Action. They humanely trapped them and released them in a park at the edge of town. Within three days, they were all back in the synagogue.

The Reform Synagogue had several lengthy meetings, including those in which all members voiced opinions. Finally they decided to vote the squirrels in as members of the Temple.

Now they only see them on Rosh Hashanah and Yom Kippur.

* * * * *

A man had just finished reading his book "Man Of The House" while making his commute home from work. By the time he reached home, he stormed into the house and walked directly up to his wife, pointing his finger in her face, he said "From now on I want you to know that I am the man of the house and my word is law! You are to prepare me a gourmet meal tonight, and when I'm finished eating my meal, I expect a scrumptious dessert afterward. Then, after dinner, you're going to draw my bath so I can relax. And when I'm finished with my bath, guess who's going to dress me and comb my hair?"

"The Funeral Director would be my guess," said his wife.

*　*　*　*　*

Top 10 movies to rent during Hanukah:

1.　Three Men and a Bubbie

2.　A Few Good Mensches

3.　The Cohenheads

4.　The Rocky Hora Picture Show

5.　Shalom Alone

6.　Goyz in the Hood

7.　A Gefilta Fish Called Wanda

8.　The Wizard Of Oys

9.　Who Framed Roger Rabbi

10.　Prelude To A Bris

*　*　*　*　*

All we ever hear are "Jewish" jokes and sometimes they grow tiresome; So here are some Gentile jokes:

A Gentile goes into a clothing store and says: "This is a very fine jacket. How much is it?"

The salesman says: "It's $500."

The Gentile says, "OK, I'll take it."

*　*　*　*　*

Two Gentiles meet on the street. The first one says, "You own your own business, don't you? How's it going?" The other Gentile says "Just great! Thanks for asking!"

*   *   *   *   *

Two Gentile mothers meet on the street and start talking about children. Gentile mother 1 (said with pride): "My son is a construction worker!" Gentile mother 2 (said with more pride): "My son is a truck driver!"

*   *   *   *   *

A Gentile man calls his mother and says, "Mother, I know you're expecting me for dinner this evening, but something important has come up and I can't make it." His mother says, "OK."

*   *   *   *   *

A Gentile couple goes to a nice restaurant. The man says, "I'll have the steak and a baked potato, and my wife will have the Julienne salad with house dressing. We'll both have coffee." The waiter says: "How would you like your steak and salad prepared?" The man says "I'd like the steak medium, the salad is fine as is." The waiter says: " Thank you."

*   *   *   *   *

A Gentile man calls his elderly mother. He asks, "Mom, how are you feeling? Do you need anything?" She says, "I feel fine, and I don't need anything. Thanks for calling."

*   *   *   *   *

A Gentile woman meets an old Gentile friend. The friend asks "How is your son getting along?" The Gentile woman says: "He's just fine. He just turned 35." "And where does he live?" asks the friend. "He lives at home with me. I don't think he'll ever get married." The friend says, "How nice."

*   *   *   *   *

Moishe, a Jewish actor is so down and out, he's ready to take any acting gig that he can find. Finally, he gets a lead, a classified ad that says, "Actor needed to play an ape."

"I could do that," says Moishe.

To his surprise, the employer turns out to be the Central Park Zoo in New York. Owing to mismanagement, the zoo has spent so much money renovating the grounds and improving the habitat, they can no longer afford to import the ape to replace the recently deceased one, so, until they can, they'll put an actor in an ape suit. - Out of desperation, Moishe takes the offer.

At first, his conscience keeps nagging him, that he is being dishonest by fooling the zoo-goers. Moishe also feels undignified in the ape suit, stared at by the crowds who watch his every move. But after a few days on the job, he begins to enjoy all the attention and starts to put on a show for all the zoo-goers. Moishe hangs upside down from the branches by his legs, swinging about on the vines, climbing up the cage walls and roaring with all his might, while beating on his chest. Soon, he's drawing a sizable crowd.

One day, when Moishe is swinging on the vines to show off to a group of school kids, his hand slips and he goes flying over the fence into the neighboring cage, the lion's den.

Terrified, Moishe backs up as far from the approaching lion as he can, covers his eyes with his paws and prays at the top of his lungs, "Shma Yisroel Adonoi Elahemu, Adonoi Achud!"

The lion opens his powerful jaws and roars the response, "Baruch Shem K'vod Malchuso L'olam Va'ed"

From a nearby cage, a panda yells, "Shut up you schmucks, you'll get us all fired."

Synagogue Bulletin Board Bloopers

Supposedly real, some very funny.

1. Don't let worry kill you. Let your synagogue help. Join us for our Oneg after services. Prayer and medication to follow. Remember in prayer the many who are sick of our congregation.

2. For those of you who have children and don't know it, we have a nursery downstairs.

3. We are pleased to announce the birth of David Weiss, the sin of Rabbi and Mrs. Abe Weiss.

4. Thursday at 9, there will be a meeting of the Little Mothers Club. All women wishing to become Little Mothers please see the Rabbi in his private study.

5. The ladies of Hadassah have cast off clothing of every kind and they may be seen in the basement on Tuesdays.

6. A bean supper will be held Wednesday evening in the community center. Music will follow.

7. Weight Watchers will meet at 7 PM at the JCC. Please use the large double doors at the side entrance.

8. Rabbi is on vacation. Massages can be given to his secretary.

9. Goldblum will be entering the hospital this week for testes.

10. The Men's Club is warmly invited to the Oneg hosted by Hadassah. Refreshments will be served for a nominal feel.

11. Please join us as we show our support for Amy and Rob, who are preparing for the girth of their first child.

12. We are taking up a collection to defray the cost of the new carpet in the sanctuary. All those wishing to do something on the carpet will come forward and get a piece of paper.

13. If you enjoy sinning, the choir is looking for you!

In Jerusalem, an American female journalist heard about an old Rabbi who visited the Wailing Wall to pray, twice a day, everyday, for a long, long time. In an effort to check out the story, she goes to the holy site and there he is! She watches the bearded old man at prayer--and after about 45 minutes, when he turns to leave, she approaches him for an interview. "I'm Rebecca Smith from CNN, sir, how long have you been coming to the Wailing Wall and praying?"

"For about 50 years," he informs her.

"50 years! That's amazing! What do you pray for?"

"I pray for peace between the Jews and the Arabs. I pray for all the hatred to stop and I pray for all our children to grow up in safety and friendship."

"And how do you feel, sir, after doing this for 50 years?"

"Like I'm talking to a damn wall."

* * * * *

A little old Jewish man shuffled into an elevator at his hotel. Just as the doors closed, a beautiful blonde with a fantastic body stepped in with him. As the elevator started up, she pushed the STOP button and turned to him, "I have always had this fantasy about making it with an older man," she said, "I want to take you up to my room and undress you slowly. When you are naked, I want to kiss you all over your body and fondle you until every thing that is soft is soft no more. Then I want to lay you down, get on top of you and give you the ride of your life. That's my fantasy. What do you say?" the old guy looked at her for a while and then asked, "What's in it for me?"

* * * * *

A woman goes to the post office to buy stamps for her Chanukah cards. She says to the clerk: "May I have 50 Chanukah stamps?"

"What denomination?" says the clerk

The woman says: "Oy vey…my God, Has it come to this? Okay, Give me 6 Orthodox, 12 Conservative, and 32 Reform."

* * * * *

The plane was encountering severe problems on a transatlantic flight. Then it got really rough. Finally the pilot - a "good ole southern boy" announced in a pronounced drawl:

"Folks… y'all can tell we're havin' trouble. We can't maintain altitude. So we'll throw all the luggage off the plane, we'll lighten the load and get outta this mess."

The luggage went out but it wasn't much better. The pilot then announced: "We're in real trouble here."

"We're still too heavy. We're gonna have to lose a few people to save all of the rest of us. The only thing I can think of is to do this … in alphabetical order. So here goes, starting with 'A'."

"Will all the African-Americans please stand up." Nobody moved.

"Will all the Blacks please stand up." Still nobody moved.

"Will all the Coloreds please stand up." Again, nobody moved.

A young Black child turned to her mother: "Mom, aren't we all of those things ?"

Her mother replied: "Nope. Today, we are Schvartzas."

Famous Jewish Mothers

MONA LISA'S JEWISH MOTHER: "This you call a smile, after all the money your father and I spent on braces?"

CHRISTOPHER COLUMBUS'S JEWISH MOTHER: "I don't care what you've discovered, you still should have written!"

MICHELANGELO'S JEWISH MOTHER: "Why can't you paint on walls like other children? Do you know how hard it is to get this junk off the ceiling?"

NAPOLEON'S JEWISH MOTHER: "All right, if you're not hiding your report card inside your jacket, take your hand out of there and show me!"

ABRAHAM LINCOLN'S JEWISH MOTHER: "Again with the hat! Why can't you wear a baseball cap like the other kids?"

GEORGE WASHINGTON'S JEWISH MOTHER: "Next time I catch you throwing money across the Potomac, you can kiss your allowance goodbye!"

THOMAS EDISON'S JEWISH MOTHER: "Of course I'm proud that you invented the electric light bulb. Now turn it off and go to sleep!"

PAUL REVERE'S JEWISH MOTHER: "I don't care where you think you have to go, young man, midnight is long past your curfew!"

And then these two, who really did have Jewish mothers:

ALBERT EINSTEIN'S JEWISH MOTHER: "But it's your senior photograph! Couldn't you have done something about your hair?"

MOSES'S JEWISH MOTHER: "That's a good story! Now tell me where you've really been for the last forty years."

Two Jewish sisters-in-law, Ruth and Golda, meet on the street. Ruth says to Golda, "Such news I got for you, Golda! My son is finally getting married. He tells me he is engaged to this wonderful Jewish girl, but he thinks the poor darling may have some strange illness called herpes."

After offering congratulations, Golda says to Ruth, "So, Ruthie, do you have any idea what is this herpes, and can he catch it?"

Ruth answers, "God forbid! But his Papa and I are just so happy to hear about his engagement. You know how we've all worried about him. It's past time he's settled with a nice girl. As far as the herpes goes, who knows?"

"Well," Golda says, "I have a very fine medical dictionary, you know, Ruthie. I'll just run home right now and look it up and call you."

So, Golda goes home, looks it up, and calls Ruth excitedly, "Ruth! Thank goodness, I found it. Not to worry! It says herpes is a disease affecting the Gentiles!"

* * * * *

God said, "Adam, I want you to do something for me."

Adam said, "Gladly, Lord, what do You want me to do?"

God said, "Go down into that valley."

Adam said, "What's a valley?"

God explained it to him.

Then God said, "Cross the river."

Adam said, "What's a river?"

God explained that to him, and then said, "Go over to the hill......."

Adam said, "What is a hill?"

So, God explained to Adam what a hill was.

He told Adam, "On the other side of the hill you will find a cave"

Adam said, "What's a cave?"

After God explained, he said, "In the cave you will find a Woman."

Adam said, "What's a woman?"

So God explained that to him, too.

Then, God said, "I want you to reproduce."

Adam said, "How do I do that?"

God first said (under his breath), "Geez....."

And then, just like everything else, God explained that to Adam, as well.

So, Adam goes down into the valley, across the river, and over the hill, into the cave, and finds the woman.

Then, in about five minutes, he was back.

God, his patience wearing thin, said angrily, "What is it now?"

And Adam said, "What's a headache?"

* * * * *

A man wonders if having sex on the Sabbath is a sin because he is not sure if sex is work or play. So he goes to a Priest and asks for his opinion on this question. After consulting the Bible, the Priest says, "My son, after an exhaustive search, I am positive that sex is work and is therefore not permitted on the Sabbath."

The man thinks: "What does a Priest know about sex?" So he goes to a Minister, who after all is a married man and experienced in this matter. He queries the Minister and receives the same reply. "Sex is work and therefore not for the Sabbath!"

Not pleased with the reply, he seeks out a Rabbi: a man of thousands of years tradition and knowledge. The Rabbi ponders the question, then states, "My son, sex is definitely play."

The man replies, "Rabbi, how can you be so sure when so many others tell me sex is work?"

The Rabbi softly speaks, "If sex were work, my wife would have the maid do it."

The Power of Prayer

Cohen showed up at synagogue one Saturday and the Rabbi almost fell down when he saw him. Cohen had never been seen in a synagogue in his life.

After Services, the Rabbi caught Cohen and said: "Mr. Cohen, I am so glad you decided to come here. What made you come?"

Cohen said, "I got to be honest with you, Rabbi, a while back, I misplaced my favorite hat and I really, really love that hat. I know that Levy had one just like mine and I knew that Levy came to Services every Saturday. I also knew that Levy takes off his hat during Services and he leaves it in the back of the sanctuary. So, I was going to leave after the Shmah and steal Levy's hat."

Later, the Rabbi said: "Well, Cohen, I notice that you didn't steal Levy's hat. What changed your mind?"

Cohen said, "Well, after I heard your sermon on the 10 commandments, I decided that I didn't need to steal Levy's hat."

The Rabbi gave Cohen a big smile and said, "After I talked about 'Thou Shalt Not Steal' you decided you would rather do without your hat than burn in Hell, right?"

Cohen shook his head and said: "Not exactly, Rabbi, after you talked about 'Thou Shalt Not Commit Adultery' I remembered where I left it."

* * * * *

Sarah, "I've been asked to get married hundreds of times."

Miriam (surprised), "Really?! By whom?"

Sarah, "My parents."

* * * * *

A young Jewish Mom walks her son to the school bus corner on his first day of kindergarten.

"Behave, my bubaleh" she says. "Take good care of yourself and think about your Mother, tataleh!"

"And come right back home on the bus, schein kindaleh." "Mommy loves you a lot, my ketsaleh!"

At the end of the school day the bus comes back and she runs to her son on and hugs him.

"So what did my pupaleh learn on his first day of school?"

The boy answers, "I've learned that my name is David."

* * * * *

Moishe meets Arnold at their social club and asks how Abe's funeral went the other day.

"It went OK, Moishe," replied Arnold, "but at the end of the Rabbi's eulogy, I had to try and stop myself from laughing aloud."

"Why was that?" asks Moishe.

"Well," says Arnold, "throughout his marriage to Miriam, she was always telling me what a mean man he was. He never had a steady job and the money he brought home to her wasn't enough for food and clothing, let alone holidays. Yet he drank heavily and often stayed out all night gambling. Altogether, a good husband he was not. But at the funeral, the Rabbi spoke of how wonderful the deceased was - so considerate, so beloved, so thoughtful to others.

78

Then, when the Rabbi had finished, I heard Miriam say to one of her children, "Do me a favor, go see whether it's your father in the coffin."

* * * * *

Morris and his wife Esther went to the state fair every year, and every year Morris would say,"Esther, I'd like to ride in that helicopter." Esther always replied, "I know Morris, but that helicopter ride is 50 dollars, and 50 dollars is 50 dollars." One year Esther and Morris went to the fair, and Morris said, "Esther I'm 85 years old. If I don't ride that helicopter, I might never get another chance." Esther replied "Morris that helicopter ride is 50 dollars, and 50 dollars is 50 dollars."

The pilot overheard the couple and said, "Folks I'll make you a deal I'll take the both of you for a ride. If you can stay quiet for the entire ride and not say a word I won't charge you! But if you say one word, it's 50 dollars".

Morris and Esther agreed and up they went. The pilot did all kinds of fancy maneuvers, but not a word was heard. He did his daredevil tricks over and over again, but still not a word. When they landed, the pilot turned to Morris and said "By golly, I did everything I could to get you to yell out, but you didn't. I'm impressed!"

Morris replied "Well, I was going to say something when Esther fell out, but 50 dollars is 50 dollars."

* * * * *

Morris died. His will provided $50,000 for an elaborate funeral.

As the last attendees left, Morris's wife Rose turned to her oldest friend Sadie and said, "Well, I'm sure Morris would be pleased with the service."

"I'm sure you're right," replied Sadie, who leaned in close and lowered her voice to a whisper. "Tell me, how much did it really cost?"

"All of it," said Rose. "Fifty thousand."

"No!" Sadie exclaimed. "I mean, it was very nice, but really... $50,000?"

Rose nodded. "The funeral was $6,500. I donated $500 to the shul for the Rabbi's services. The shiva food and drinks were another $500. The rest went for the memorial stone."

Sadie computed quickly. "$42,500 for a memorial stone? Oy vey, how big is it?"

"Five and a half carats."

* * * * *

A young boy is looking at the memorial placque on the wall in a hall of the temple. He notices the little lights on next to some of the names and wonders why these lights are on.

Just then, the Rabbi walks by, and the child asks why these names have lights on next to them.

The Rabbi says, "These are men who died in the service."

The boy asks, "Rosh Hashanah or Yom Kippur?"

* * * * *

The Wise Old Rabbi....

A Jewish woman goes to see her Rabbi..

"Two men are in love with me," she says. "Who will be the lucky one?"

The wise old Rabbi says, "Abe will marry you. Sol will be the lucky one."

* * * * *

A man walked into the lingerie department of a local retail store. He told the saleslady that he would like a Jewish bra for his wife, size 34B.

With a quizzical look the saleslady asked, "What kind of bra?"

He repeated, "A Jewish bra. She said to tell you that she wanted a Jewish bra, and that you would know what she wanted."

The saleslady replied, "We don't get as many requests for them as we used to. Most of our customers lately want the Catholic bra, or the Salvation Army bra, or the Presbyterian bra."

Confused and a little flustered, the man asked "So, what are the differences?"

The saleslady responded. "It is all really quite simple. The Catholic bra supports the masses. The Salvation Army lifts up the fallen, and the Presbyterian bra keeps them staunch and upright."

He mused on that information for a minute and said: "Hmmm. I know I'll regret asking, but what does the Jewish bra do?"

"Ah, the Jewish bra," she replied, "makes mountains out of molehills.

* * * * *

A Jew was walking on Regent Street in London and stopped at a posh gourmet food shop. An impressive salesperson in morning coat with tails approached him and politely asked, "May I help you, Sir?"

"Yes," replied the customer, "I would like to buy a pound of lox."

"No. No," responded the dignified salesperson, "You mean smoked salmon."

"Okay, a pound of smoked salmon."

"Anything else?"

"Yes, a dozen blintzes."

"No. No. You mean crepes."

"Okay, a dozen crepes."

"Anything else?"

"Yes. A pound of chopped liver."

"No. No. You mean pate."

"Okay," said the Jewish patron, "A pound of pate. And," he added, "I'd like you to deliver this to my house next Saturday."

"Look," retorted the indignant salesperson, "We don't schlep on Shabbos."

* * * * *

KOSHER COMPUTER

Made in Israel by DELLSHALOM. It is selling at such a good price!! If you or a friend are considering a Kosher computer, you should know that there are some important upgrades and changes from the typical computer you are used to, such as:

The cursor moves from right to left.

Microsoft Office now includes, "A little byte of this, and a little byte of that."

It comes with two hard drives-one for fleyshedik business software and one for milchedik games.

Instead of getting a "General Protection Fault" error, my PC now gets "Ferklempt."

The Chanukah screen savers include "Flying Dreidels".

The PC also shuts down automatically at sundown on Friday evenings.

The "Start" button has been replaced with the "Let's Go!! I'm Not Getting Any Younger!" button.

When disconnecting external devices from the back of my PC, you are instructed to "Remove the cable from the PC's tuchus."

Internet Explorer has a spinning "Star of David" in the upper right corner.

You will hear "Hava Nagila" during startup.

When running "ScanDisk," it prompts with a "You want I should fix this?" message.

When your PC is working too hard, I occasionally hear a loud "Oy!!!"

Year 2000" issues were replaced by "Year 5760-5761" issues.

After 20 minutes of no activity, your PC would go "Schloffen."

Computer viruses would now be cured with chicken soup.

There is a "monitor cleaning solution" from Manischewitz that advertises that it gets rid of the "schmutz und drek" on your monitor.

After your computer dies, you MUST dispose of it within 24 hours.

And of course the BEST Feature of all:

Kosher Computers DONT GET SPAM!

* * * * *

A Jewish man picked up the phone and dialed. When a voice answered, he asked, "Mother, how are you?"

"Fine."

"Sorry, I have the wrong number."

* * * * *

The trouble with some Jewish women is that they get all excited about nothing and then they marry him.

* * * * *

A Bar Mitzvah is defined as the day when a Jewish boy comes to the realization that he is more likely to own a professional sports team than he is to play for one.

Holiday Distinctions

1. Christmas is one day, same day every year: December 25th Jews also love December 25th. It's another paid day off. We go to movies and out for Chinese food. Chanukah is 8 days. It starts the evening of the 24th of Kislev, whenever that falls. No one is ever sure. Jews never know until a non-Jewish friend asks when Chanukah starts, forcing us to consult a calendar so we don't look like idiots. We all have the same calendar, provided free with a donation from either the World Jewish Congress, the kosher butcher, or the local Sinai Memorial Chapel (especially in Florida) or other Jewish funeral home.

2. Christmas is a major holiday. Chanukah is a minor holiday with the same theme as most Jewish holidays. They tried to kill us, we survived, let's eat.

3. Christians get wonderful presents such as jewelry, perfume or stereos. Jews get practical presents such as underwear, socks, or the collected works of the Rambam, which looks impressive on the bookshelf.

4. There is only one way to spell Christmas. No one can decide how to spell Chanukah, Chanukah, Chanukka, Channukah, Hanukah, Hannukah.

5. Christmas is a time of great pressure for husbands and boyfriends. Their partners expect special gifts. Jewish men are relieved of that burden. No one expects a diamond ring on Chanukah.

6. Christmas brings enormous electric bills. Candles are used for Chanukah. Not only are we spared enormous electric bills, but we get to feel good about not contributing to the energy crisis.

7. Christmas carols are beautiful. Silent Night, Come All Ye Faithful.... Chanukah songs are about dreidels made from clay or

having a party and dancing the horah. Of course, we are secretly pleased that many of the beautiful carols were composed and written by our tribal brethren. And don't Barbra Streisand and Neil Diamond sing them beautifully?

8. A home preparing for Christmas smells wonderful. The sweet smell of cookies and cakes baking. Happy people are gathered around in festive moods. A home preparing for Chanukah smells of oil, potatoes, and onions. The home, as always, is full of loud people all talking at once.

9. Women have fun baking Christmas cookies. Women burn their eyes and cut their hands grating potatoes and onions for latkas on Chanukah. Another reminder of our suffering through the ages.

10. Parents deliver presents to their children during Christmas. Jewish parents have no qualms about withholding a gift on any of the eight nights.

11. The players in the Christmas story have easy to pronounce names such as Mary, Joseph, and Jesus. The players in the Chanukah story are Antiochus, Judah Maccabee, and Matta whatever. No one can spell it or pronounce it. On the plus side, we can tell our friends anything and they believe we are wonderfully versed in our history.

12. In recent years, Christmas has become more and more commercialized. The same holds true for Chanukah, even though it is a minor holiday. It makes sense. How could we market a major holiday such as Yom Kippur? Forget about celebrating. Think observing. Come to synagogue, starve yourself for hours, become one with your dehydrated soul, beat your chest, confess your sins, a guaranteed good time for you and your family. Tickets a mere $200 per person. Better stick with Chanukah!

Better stick with Chanukah!

A Jewish congregation in New York honors its Rabbi for 25 years of service by sending him to Hawaii for a week, all expenses paid.

When he walks into his hotel room, there's a beautiful girl, nude, lying on the bed. She says, "Hi, Rabbi, I'm a little something extra that the president of the board arranged for you."

The Rabbi is incensed. He picks up the phone, calls the President of the Temple Board and says, "Greenberg, what were you thinking? Where's your respect? I am the moral leader of our community! I am very angry with you and you have not heard the end of this."

The girl gets up and starts to get dressed. The Rabbi turns to her and says, "Where are you going? I'm not angry with you."

Jewish Wisdom

1. Twenty percent off is a bargain; fifty percent off is a mitzvah.

2. If you don't eat, it will kill your mother and grandmother.

3. Anything worth saying is worth repeating a thousand times.

4. Prune Danish is an acquired taste.

5. No meal is complete without leftovers.

6. Virtually all Jewish wisdom is somehow related to food.

* * * * *

Cultural Perspective:

The Italian says, "I'm tired and thirsty. I must have wine."

The Frenchman says, "I'm tired and thirsty. I must have cognac."

The Russian says, "I'm tired and thirsty. I must have vodka."

The German says, "I'm tired and thirsty. I must have beer."

The Mexican says, "I'm tired and thirsty. I must have tequila."

The Jew says, "I'm tired and thirsty. I must have diabetes."

* * * * *

Doctor Bloom who was known for miraculous cures for arthritis had a waiting room full of people when a little old lady, completely bent over in half, shuffled in slowly, leaning on her cane. When her turn came, she went into the doctor's office, and, amazingly, emerged within half an hour walking completely erect with her head held high.

A woman in the waiting room who had seen all this walked up to the little old lady and said, "It's a miracle! You walked in bent in half and now you're walking erect. What did that doctor do?"

She answered, "Miracle, shmiracle .. he gave me a longer cane."

* * * * *

"Hello is this the Goldberg residence?"

"Yes, mit whom do you vish to speak?"

"Mrs. Goldberg please?"

"Mrs. Goyeldberg is shoppink in de supermarket"

"Is Mr. Goldberg there?"

"Dis time of de day? Mishter Goyeldberg is voikink"

"Is Thelma at home?"

"In de school is Telma, very clever vun, tu tu tu"

"How about Harry, is he there?"

"Herry, in colletch is Herry, he should be a dokter kaynahoreh"

"I see, is this Mrs Goldberg mother?"

"No, Poor Bubbi Goyeldberg is ollivasholom"

"So, may I ask who I am talking to?"

"Dis is Daisy, de Shvartza!"

* * * * *

Test Your Yiddish Skills

(answers are at the end)

1) Which one of these people might best be described as "zoftig?"

   A) Callista Flockhart

   B) Lara Flynn Boyle

   C) Kirstie Alley

   D) Woody Allen

2) You're driving around in eckveldt (the boondocks) and have no idea where you are. You are:

   A) farblunget

   B) farklempt

   C) fartoost

   D) farshvitzed

3) You found it! The Holy Grail! A $2000 designer dress for just $39.95! You've found a:

   A) mechaiyeh

   B) mishpucheh

   C) machashafer

   D) metziah

4) Which one of these people has a "ferbisseneh punim?"

A) Michael Jackson

B) Leona Helmsley

C) Barbara Walters

D) Julia Roberts

5) He eats like a pig and wipes his face with the back of his hand. He farts and picks his nose at the dinner table. He curses like a drunken sailor. He's a real:

A) shnorror

B) gonif

C) grubber yung

D) mensch

6) Which of these is NOT a body part?

A) poulkie

B) potchki

C) pupik

D) punim

7) Which of these is NOT an insult:

A) shana maydel

B) shmegeggie

C) shmendrik

D) shlub

8) You've gone to a wild party where you've been downing vodka shots like candy. You can barely stand up anymore, and you've made a fool of yourself in front of everyone you know. You are totally, completely:

A) fershtayst

B) farblunget

C) ferchadded

D) fershikert

9) Which of these things would you never find at a kosher restaurant?

A) shmaltz

B) luckshen kugel

C) treyf

D) kasha varnishkes

10) Of these various uses of "kishka", which one is incorrect?

A) "Yes, waiter. I'll have the roast chicken with a side order of kishka."

B) "That Yetta, she's such a piece of kishka!"

C) "After twenty years of keeping secrets, he finally went to a shrink and spilled his kishkas."

D) "If anyone ever tried to mug me, boy, I'd give him such a chamalyiah in the kishkas!"

Answers to Quiz:

Question 1 = C

Question 2 = A

Question 3 = D

Question 4 = B

Question 5 = C

Question 6 = B

Question 7 = A

Question 8 = D

Question 9 = C

Question 10 = B

An elderly Jewish man approached a very beautiful young woman in Wal-Mart.

"Excuse me," he said, "I've lost my wife somehow. Can you talk to me for a couple of minutes?"

The woman, feeling a bit of compassion for the old fellow said, "Certainly, Sir. Do you know where your wife might be?"

"I have no idea, but every time I talk to a beautiful young woman with tits like yours, my wife appears out of nowhere."

*　*　*　*　*

Six retired Floridians were playing poker in the condo clubhouse when Meyerwitz lost $500 on a single hand, clutched his chest and dropped dead, still sitting at the table.

Showing respect for their fallen comrade, the other five continue playing standing up.

Finkelstein looks around and asked, "So, who's gonna tell his wife?"

They cut the cards. Goldberg picks the two of clubs and has to carry the news.

They tell him to be discreet, be gentle, don't make a bad situation any worse.

"Discreet? I'm the most discreet person you'll ever meet. Discretion is my middle name. Leave it to me."

Goldberg goes over to the Meyerwitz apartment and knocks on the door.

The wife answers thru the door and asks what he wants?

Goldberg declares: "Your husband just lost $500 in a poker game and is afraid to come home."

"Tell him to drop dead!" yells the wife.

"I'll go tell him." Says Goldberg.

* * * * *

Three men were sitting around bragging about how they had given their new wives duties.

The first man had married a Catholic woman, and bragged that he had told his wife she was to do all the dishes and house cleaning that needed doing at their house. He said it took a couple days, but on the third day he came home to a clean house and the dishes were all washed and put away.

The second man had married a Mormon woman. He bragged that he had given his wife orders that she was to do all the cleaning, the dishes and the cooking. He told them the first day he didn't see any results, but the next day it was better. By the third day, his house was clean, the dishes were done, and he had a huge dinner on the table.

The third man had married a Jewish girl. He boasted that he told her that her duties were to keep the house clean, dishes washed, lawn mowed, laundry done and hot meals on the table, every day. He said the first day he didn't see anything, the second day he didn't see anything, but by the third day most of the swelling had gone down and he could see a little out of his left eye.

* * * * *

Several centuries ago, the Pope decreed that all the Jews had to convert or leave Italy.

There was a huge outcry from the Jewish community, so the Pope offered a deal. He would have a religious debate with the leader of the Jewish community. If the Jews won, they could stay in Italy, if the Pope won, they would have to convert or leave.

The Jewish people met and picked an aged but wise Rabbi Moishe to represent them in the debate. However, as Moishe spoke no Italian and the Pope spoke no Yiddish, they all agreed that it would be a "silent" debate.

On the chosen day, the Pope and Rabbi Moishe sat opposite each other for a full minute before the Pope raised his hand and showed three fingers. Rabbi Moishe looked back and raised one finger. Next, the Pope waved his finger around his head. Rabbi Moishe pointed to the ground where he sat. The Pope then brought out a communion wafer and a chalice of wine. Rabbi Moishe pulled out an apple. With that, the Pope stood up and declared that he was beaten, that Rabbi Moishe was too clever, and that the Jews could stay.

Later, the Cardinals met with the Pope, asking what had happened. The Pope said, "First, I held up three fingers to represent the Trinity. He responded by holding up one finger to remind me that there is still only one God common to both our beliefs. Then, I waved my finger to show him that God was all around us. He responded by pointing to the ground to show that God was also right here with us. I pulled out the wine and wafer to show that God absolves us of all our sins. He pulled out an apple to remind me of original sin. He had me beaten and I couldn't continue."

Meanwhile the Jewish community gathered around Rabbi Moishe. "How did you win the debate?" they asked. "I haven't a clue," said Moishe. "First he said to me that we had three days to get out of Italy, so I gave him the finger. Then he tells me that the whole country would be cleared of Jews and I said to him, we're staying right here." "And then what?" asked a woman. "Who knows?" said Moishe, "He took out his lunch, so I took out mine."

* * * * *

A man walks into a shul with a dog. The shammas comes up to him and says, "Pardon me, this is a House of Worship, you can't bring your dog in here."

"What do you mean," says the man, "this is a Jewish dog. Look."

And the shammas looks carefully and sees that in the same way that a St. Bernard carries a brandy barrel round its neck this dog has a tallis bag round its neck.

"Rover," says the man, "kipa!".

"Woof!" says the dog, stands on his hind legs, opens the tallis bag, takes out a kipa and puts it on his head.

"Rover," says the man, "tallis!".?

"Woof!" says the dog, stands on his hind legs, opens the tallis bag, takes out a tallis and puts it round his neck.

"Rover," says the man, "daven!".

"Woof!" says the dog, stands on his hind legs, opens the tallis bag, takes out a siddur and starts to daven.

"That's fantastic," says the shammas, "absolutely amazing, incredible! You should take him to Hollywood, get him on television, get him in the movies, you could make a million dollars off of him!!"

"You speak to him," says the man, "He wants to be a doctor!"

* * * * *

In a large Florida city, the Rabbi developed quite a reputation for impressive sermons, so much so, that everyone who was Jewish in the community came every Shabbat.

Unfortunately, one weekend a member had to visit Long Island for his nephew's bar mitzvah, but he didn't want to miss the Rabbi's sermon. So he decided to hire a Shabbat goy to sit in the congregation and tape the sermon so he could listen to it when he returned.

Other congregants saw what was going on, and they also decided to hire Shabbat goys to tape the sermon so they could play golf instead of going to Shul.

Within a few weeks time there were 500 gentiles sitting in Shul taping the Rabbi. The Rabbi got wise to this. The following Shabbat he, too, hired a Shabbat goy who brought a tape recorder to play his prerecorded sermon to the 500 Gentiles in the congregation who dutifully recorded his words on their machines...

... Marking the first incidence in history of artificial insermonation.

* * * * *

An elderly man in Miami called his son in New York and said, "I hate to ruin your day, but I have to tell you that your mother and I are divorcing. Forty-five years of misery is enough."

"Pop, what are you talking about?" the son screamed.

"We can't stand the sight of each other any longer," the old man said. "We're sick of each other, and I'm sick of talking about this, so you call your sister in Chicago and tell her," and he hung up.

Frantic, the son called his sister, who exploded on the phone, "They are not getting divorced," she shouts, "I'll take care of this."

She called her father immediately and screamed at the old man, "You are NOT getting divorced! Don't do a single thing until I get there. I'm calling my brother back, and we'll both be there tomorrow. Until then, don't do a thing; DO YOU HEAR ME?" and hung up.

The old man hung up his phone, smiled, and turned to his wife...

"Okay," he said, "They're coming for Passover and paying their own airfares."

You knew you were Jewish if...

+ You watched Ed Sullivan every Sunday night, and your parents laughed out loud at Myron Cohen (if you don't know who Myron Cohen is, don't bother reading any further).

+ You spent your entire childhood thinking everyone called pot roast "brisket."

+ Your family dog responded to commands in Yiddish.

+ You had at least one female relative who penciled on eyebrows which were always asymmetrical.

+ You were as tall as your grandmother by the age of seven.

+ You were as tall as your grandfather by the age seven and a half.

+ You never knew anyone whose last name didn't end in one of 5 standard suffixes (berg, baum, man, stein and witz.)

+ You were surprised to discover that wine doesn't always taste like cranberry sauce.

+ You can look at gefilte fish and not turn green.

+ When your mother smacked you, she continued to make you feel bad for hurting her hand.

+ You know how to pronounce numerous Yiddish words and use them correctly in context, yet you don't exactly know what they mean. Kinaynahora.

+ You considered your Bar or Bat Mitzvah a "Get Out of Hebrew School Free" card.

- You're compelled to mention your grandmother's "clunkers" or "cannonballs" upon seeing fluffy matzo balls served at restaurants.

- Your mother or grandmother took personal pride when a Jew was noted for some accomplishment (showbiz, medicine, politics, etc.) and was ashamed and embarrassed when a Jew was accused of a crime .. as if they were relatives.

- And finally, you knew that Sunday night and the night after any Jewish holiday was designated for Chinese food.

- You thought pasta was stuff used exclusively for kugel and kasha with bowties.

- You can understand Yiddish but you can't speak it.

- You're still angry at your parents for not speaking both Yiddish and English to you when you were a baby.

- You have at least one ancestor who is somehow related to your spouse's ancestor.

- Your grandparent's newly washed linoleum floor was covered with the NY Times, which your grandparents could not read.

- You thought speaking loud was normal.

- You think eating half a jar of dill pickles is a wholesome snack.

- You buy 3 shopping bags worth of hot bagels on every trip to NYC and ship them home via FedEx. (Or, if you live near NYC or Philadelphia or another Jewish city hub, you drive 3 hours just to buy a dozen "real" bagels.)

- You thought sleepaway college was only where non-Jews went ... Jews went to city schools ... unless they had scholarships or made an Ivy League school.

Thoughts On Growing Up In A Jewish Home

Isn't it redundant to put a yarmulke on a toupee?

Yiddish word for Today: PULKES (PUHL-kees) THIGHS note: this word has been traced back to the language of one of the original Tribes of Israel, the Cellulites.

When you say some English words with a Yiddish accent, they take on a whole new meaning. For example, if you would have asked my dad what the word wrench meant, he would have said something like: "A wrench is where cowboys keep their horses."

The only good advice your Jewish mother gave you was, "Go! You might meet somebody!"

You grew up thinking it was normal for someone to shout "Are you okay?" through the bathroom door when you were in there longer than 3 minutes.

Every Sunday morning your father went to the neighborhood deli (called an appetitizing store) for whitefish salad, whitefish ("chubs"), lox (nova if you were rich!), herring, corned beef, roast beef, coleslaw, potato salad, a ½-dozen huge barrel pickles which you reached into the brine for, a dozen assorted bagels, cream cheese and rye bread (sliced while he waited).

Every Sunday afternoon was spent visiting your grandparents and/or other relatives.

You may have experienced the phenomenon of 50 people fitting into a 10-foot-wide dining room hitting each other with plastic plates trying to get to a deli tray.

Signs posted on Synagogue Bulletin Boards

1. Under same management for over 5763 years.

2. Don't give up. Moses was once a basket case.

3. What part of "Thou shalt not" don't you understand?

4. Shul committees should be made up of three members, two of whom should be absent at every meeting.

* * * * *

Sign over the urinal in a bathroom at Hebrew University: "The future of the Jewish people is in your hands."

* * * * *

My mother is a typical Jewish mother. Once she was on jury duty. They sent her home. She insisted SHE was guilty.

* * * * *

Each time a person goes into a delicatessen and orders a pastrami on white bread, somewhere a Jew dies.

* * * * *

It was mealtime during a flight on El Al. "Would you like dinner?," the flight attendant asked Moshe, seated in front. "What are my choices?," Moshe asked. "Yes or no," she replied.

* * * * *

A Rabbi was opening his mail one morning. Taking a single sheet of paper form an envelope he found written on it only one word: "schmuck." At the next Friday night service, the Rabbi announced, "I have known many people who have written letters and forgot to sign their names, but this week I received a letter from someone who signed his name... and forgot to write a letter."

*　*　*　*　*

10. Three Jewish women get together for lunch. As they are being seated in the restaurant, one takes a deep breath and gives a long, slow "Oy." The second takes a deep breath as well and lets out a long, slow "Oy." The third takes a deep breath and says impatiently, "Girls, I thought we agreed that we weren't going to talk about our children."

HELLO...?? **GOD...???**ı

Can You Hear Me Now?

On a cell phone at the Wailing Wall

The Collectors

Arnie is a retired Engineer, still an avid skier at 77, active in MIT alumni affairs and a Masters in History candidate at the Harvard Extension School. He was recently awarded the Bronze Beaver, MIT's most prestigious award to an alumnus.

Alan, a virtual child at 72 is a retired Radiologist. Since retirement he has volunteer taught Tufts University medical students on rotation in Radiology at N.E. Medical Center, consulted and volunteered for the Executive Service Corps and been a guide for Boston By Foot. He has led courses at the Harvard Institute for Learning in Retirement and Lifelong Learning at Regis College on Civil War – Boston and co-led a course on Great American Fortunes (i.e. Vanderbilt, Astor, Rockefeller) with Jules Schwartz, former Dean of the Business School at Boston University. Jules discussed how they made their fortunes and Alan discussed how they spent it.

They both are married, with adult children, and have been taking courses at the Harvard Institute for Learning in Retirement and have been sharing e-mails and playing poker together with a group of distinguished card mavens.

www.ingramcontent.com/pod-product-compliance
Lightning Source LLC
Chambersburg PA
CBHW020306290526
45784CB00003B/1390